D1179135

HAPPY
VEGAN

For Eric Findlay

FEARNE COTTON

HAPPY VEGAN

SEVEN DIALS

CONTENTS

Hello from My Kitchen!   6
My Store Cupboard   8

STARTING THE DAY RIGHT   12
SNACKS   38
LUNCH ON THE GO   60
LONG AND LAZY   88
DISHY DINNERS   116
SHARING FEASTS   142
PARTY TIME   166
THE SWEETEST THING   188

Tips and Tricks   216
Acknowledgements   218
Index   219

HELLO FROM MY KITCHEN!

I have been a bit nervous to write this introduction. Food is such a personal matter and I know it can cause rifts, judgement – and sometimes even emphatic disagreement! But I'm going to put that mixing bowl of worries to one side so I can make this book a pure celebration of food. A missive of love, adoration and huge appreciation. A love song to all the combinations and concoctions that fill me with energy and joy.

After all, I can only tell you my truth and share with you my preferences, which in turn I hope you'll enjoy and perhaps be inspired by. As the title of this book might have given away, I have found a balanced way of eating that works for me and my lifestyle, and much of this involves cooking and eating vegan. I adore the vibrancy and versatility of vegan food and have loved learning and experimenting over the years with the plethora of ways in which you can create such alchemy without going anywhere near an egg. Cooking like this has given me energy, opened up my eyes to the versatility of vegetables, fruits and legumes, and has led me to research the many ways in which eating vegan can help the planet too. This book is a collection of those recipes that I love cooking for friends, eating with family and snacking on continuously in between.

As many of you might know, I have a beautifully hectic family life with two small children, sometimes two teenage children and always one very hungry husband. So these recipes are family-friendly, easy to bung together, filling to the max and made with ingredients you can bag in your local supermarket. We're not fancy in the Cotton–Wood household, but we do bloody love good food.

Here's the disclaimer bit: whilst this book is 100 per cent vegan, I'm not. I am perhaps 90 per cent as I bake with eggs quite frequently, eat the odd omelette and occasionally devour chunks of cheese. My food story begins when I, aged 12, sat watching a *Newsround* report on live animal transportation. Being a pretty strong-willed almost-teen, I encouraged my mum to ditch the meat too and overnight we cruised into vegetarianism. Bear in mind this was the early nineties when there was little in the way of encouragement or supermarket convenience to live in like this. There were a lot of Margherita pizzas for dinner and jacket potatoes for lunch and trips to friends' houses after school where parents would look exasperated as they scanned their freezers of chicken nuggets and fish fingers. Tofu was yet to shine in the mainstream spotlight and I'm pretty sure if I had heard the word batted about back then I would have assumed it was a breed of small dog.

At 21, I was in the thick of a very high-octane and exciting part of my career where I would often find myself sat in a diner in mid-America whilst filming or living off trays of sandwiches on set late at night. I was tired and finding my vegetarian lifestyle was still not as widespread or as accepted as I had hoped. I started to introduce just a little fish into my diet to help widen my options for much-needed protein, although I felt some real guilt around this switch-up.

More recently I have once again gone back to being a straight-up vegetarian mainly because our seas are being so overfished. But I still cook with meat, fish, dairy and eggs for my children as I want them to make that decision for themselves later down the line, and I also have a very fussy red-headed three-year-old mega babe whose intake of food I really can't afford to limit at this point in time. So while I might cook vegan for me and Jesse a lot of the time, I still cook classic non-vegan family favourites for my kids and stepchildren. I'm yet to convince my 17-year-old stepson to get on board with tofu (I'll get there one day!)

I guess the reason I'm confessing all this is that I want to say I believe it's okay to eat vegan all of the time, most of the time, some of the time – whatever! It's a lifestyle choice after all. I am not perfect and am certainly not writing this book to be preachy or pushy with food. I simply want to celebrate the vegan recipes that I so love cooking and certainly adore eating, and I personally believe there are some real benefits to eating this way.

It's also a great time to be giving it a go. Unlike when I went veggie in the nineties, veganism is now so popular that restaurants, takeaway places and supermarkets give us many more options, and whilst some of the posher ingredients have a price tag, for the most part it's a cheaper way of eating (considering meat, fish and cheese are some of the most expensive ingredients you can put in your trolley).

If you're a little worried that you won't consume enough protein or iron in your diet by making a fully vegan switch-up – you're in good company! I've always been very aware of this so I have been extremely conscious of including recipes in this book that cover all of our nutritional needs. Recipes packed with the above, plus colour and vitamins and tons of fibre. Meals that will see you pumped with energy and ready for whatever craziness the day throws your way. Eating vegan isn't about cutting loads of stuff out from your diet – in fact I really hope this book introduces some new store cupboard essentials to your life.

Whether you're a fully-fledged and dedicated vegan, someone that eats vegan when cooking at home but veers off when out and about, or completely new to vegan food, I hope you enjoy the process of recreating these recipes and ultimately of eating the finished result.

VIVA LA VEGAN...

If you are new to vegan food, feel overwhelmed cooking in a new way or simply don't know what the hell nutritional yeast is, then you've come to the right page.

This store cupboard section will help you identify what is needed in your kitchen cupboards at all times to make cooking these recipes a breeze. It will also reveal which ingredients will help you add a little flavour, heart and soul to your meals so you can start experimenting in new and exciting vegan ways.

PROTEIN AND FIBRE SOURCES

Beans and pulses

The humble bean makes up a big portion of necessary protein for vegans and often vegetarians too. If you're new to cooking with them or believe you don't like them, don't be put off. They're incredibly versatile and work well in savoury and, surprisingly, sweet dishes too.

So, what's all the hype about? For a start there are so many different beans that add a unique flavour, texture and colour to recipes. Here are a few you'll see throughout this book that you'll be making good friends with:

KIDNEY BEANS
Dark red in colour to add a little jewel-like quality to stews and casseroles and packed with amino acids, which are the chemicals that combine to form protein and help build our muscles. Great for your digestion and gut health too.

BLACK BEANS
These gals are great for baking as the flavour really works with chocolate, so it's a good way of adding protein to usually carb- and sugar-laden dishes. They work well with smoky flavours so perfect for chillis and stews too. Beans contain folate so using them in dishes can help you to fight fatigue and gain strength physically. Black beans actually have more fibre and

magnesium than other beans so are well worth making friends with.

BUTTER BEANS

The big daddy of the bean world offers a softer, silkier texture and again works so well in many dishes from quinoa plates to salads. They're delicate in flavour and give you that amazing much needed protein and boost of antioxidants.

HARICOT BEANS

If you fancy making your own baked beans, these are the beans for you. They're small and compact but have the same amount of goodness within. Marry them with most flavours and they'll boost your energy levels for the day.

RED, GREEN OR BROWN

These tiny little munchkins are powerful so if you don't already include them in your diet, now is your chance. They contain protein, fibre, folate, magnesium which is great for sleep, and many needed vitamins. They're great for your digestion and gut health, your energy levels and your brain. Perfect for soups, casseroles or salads, all of which you'll find in this book.

All of the beans and pulses used in these recipes can be bought precooked in cans or packets, which makes them a super easy and practical ingredient to use. Of course, if you have the time to soak the dry versions overnight, then do! But if you're short on time, then stock up on some tins – they're affordable and taste just as good!

Tofu

I adore tofu and am usually on a crusade to try to convince naysayer mates to do so too, as well as my children who constantly turn their noses up at it. But tofu remains one of the most versatile ingredients so get ready to make it your friend! You can fry it, sear it, grill it, bake it, blend silken tofu into puds and add so many varying flavours to make it really come alive.

For any recipes that use firm tofu (so not silken), make sure you drain it first. You can do this by pressing the tofu block wrapped in a clean tea towel and between two plates with a weight on top, up to a half hour before you start cooking. This ensures all the moisture is removed and the tofu won't fall apart when you use it. It's also worth knowing that you can buy smoked tofu in most supermarkets now alongside the normal variety. Smoked tofu has a wonderful umami flavour that even the most defiant of meat-eaters will find mouthwatering – if you're on the fence about tofu, make sure you give this type a go before writing it off completely.

As well as being easy to incorporate into many delicious meals it is so very good for us. It's packed with amino acids and protein and it also contains iron (which many of us are deficient in), magnesium, zinc, minerals and vitamins. Its complex combination of goodness helps to lower cholesterol too. Tofu is an all-round good egg . . . without any egg!

Nuts and seeds

You'll see many different types of nuts and seeds used throughout this book in recipes ranging from crackers and breads, to salads and chocolate squares. Eaten in moderation these natural wonders help to boost our protein levels, keep us fuller for longer and energised in the right, balanced way. As well as all of the nuts and seeds that you'll be more than aware of, this book also features flax seeds which you may not normally buy in your weekly shop. Also known as linseed, you can buy them either whole or ground into a rough powder which is a good way of getting them into food quickly if you're baking or want a little added fibre on top of your brekkie in the morning. As well as flax being a brilliant form of dietary fibre, it's also loaded with nutrients, high in omega 3 good fats and packed with protein. Omega 3 is so needed in all of our diets: it not only helps our bodies function but massively helps our brains work too. It has been said that it can even help with anxiety and depression if eaten regularly. Never underestimate the power of the flax!

Milks and yoghurts

For a lot of us, giving up cow's milk in our teas and coffees might seem like an unbearable thought but don't panic! There are so many dairy-free alternatives available now you'll definitely find one that makes your cuppa taste just as good (if not better!). In this book, I've used a mix of soya, oat, coconut, almond, cashew and rice milk but if you have a favourite already, feel free to substitute it whenever you like. If you've never ventured into the wonderful world of dairy-free milks, then next time you're at the supermarket, pick one at random and give it a go. I find that coconut milk is the most versatile since it works so well in both savoury and sweet dishes, but oat milk has a creamy texture that is great for any beginner vegans.

There are also an increasing number of vegan yoghurts available and a dollop of these really add the perfect finishing touch to lots of dishes. Like the milk, I'm a big fan of coconut milk yoghurt but there are also several soya milk yoghurts available now.

INGREDIENTS FOR FLAVOUR

Miso paste

Why, oh, why did I not discover this dreamy situation sooner? Miso paste only came into my life about three years ago and I've never looked back. It is made of fermented soya beans so has its own great nutritional value, and is a traditional Japanese seasoning product used in many dishes. I love to experiment with it, so you'll see me use it in this book for savoury and even sweet dishes. Its flavour is strangely malleable so can at times add a cheesy quality to vegan dishes which would traditionally have dairy in them, yet also a caramel quality when used correctly in sweet sauces and desserts. Get ready to embrace the miso!

Nutritional yeast

This is not your usual yeast. Don't confuse it with bread yeast as it's a totally different beast. It's a deactivated yeast which has a strong flavour perfect for vegan dishes. It can taste quite cheesy so is great if you're making 'cheese' out of nuts, or a cheesy flavoured sauce for a meal. Not only does it offer up a lot of flavour for vegan recipes, it is full of goodness; B complex vitamins can be found here as well as a little protein,

so get sprinkling and adding where necessary.

If you can't find nutritional yeast at your local shop, chances are you have a pot of yeast extract in your cupboard (you either love it, or hate it, right?) and this will have a similar effect on the flavour of your dish, so don't be afraid to get experimenting and add some to any meal that you think could do with a cheesy dimension!

Non-refined sugars

It's not necessary to cut out refined sugars on a vegan diet but it's not a bad idea to avoid them if you can. I try to avoid white sugars as they create a spike in our blood sugar and usually make me feel pretty crummy. You can get equal levels of sweetness and actually a lot more flavour by using coconut sugar or maple syrup. You won't find any honey in this book as it's not vegan. (A little fact for you: did you know it takes 20,000 bees to make one jar of honey? Incredible creatures.) But you'll find plenty of great recipes using natural sweetness from the aforementioned options as well as dates and dried apricots, and if you do eat honey then you could swap it for the maple syrup in any of the recipes.

I've always had a huge love affair with breakfast – it's often one of the first thoughts that pops into my head when my sleep-deprived eyes open. My first thought might be 'coffee' or 'why can't my kids lie in a little longer?' But it'll shortly be followed by 'FOOD!'

The morning is the most important part of the day in so many ways. I like to say hello to it by setting an intention. I'm a strange contradiction of someone that is a bit of an old hippy, yet slightly neurotic and pedantic about my routine; a free-spirited organiser, if you will. Isn't that an oxymoron? My intention could be to be more patient, to be more in the moment, to look up rather than down at my phone. It'll be different every day but the notion of having this firm thought when awakening gives me the opportunity to start as I mean to go on.

It is very much the same with food. If I start the day right nutritionally, I'll have a much better chance of finishing it that way too. That doesn't mean it's boring, lacking in any way or monotonous throughout the week. It just means what I prepare or cook and eat has perhaps had a little thought put in to it and will be enjoyed as I savour every flavour and embrace every ounce of energy it's going to give me to spring into a new 24 hours.

On weekdays my mornings are a whirlwind, like many of yours will be too, but I will always make sure amongst the shouting about school shoes and packing of school bags that the whole family eats well and is fuelled up for the day ahead. Sometimes if I have a horrendously early start at work because I'm covering for Zoe Ball on Radio 2, I will make a little something the night before to take in with me in one of my much loved airtight plastic boxes, like the Pear and pecan Bircher muesli (page 14) which is low effort but high in yum. I try to do whatever it takes to get the good stuff in me and to avoid a shop-bought, overly processed option.

If you're new to veganism and you're a passionate egg devourer in the morning and can't bear the thought of ditching your Benedicts or dippy soldiers then why not try some of the vegan alternatives in this chapter? I just love the Miso scrambled tofu and avocado on rye (page 28) which is unbelievably similar to the real thing. These options might then become firm favourites which you can alternate with, or substitute for, your usual eggy delights.

You'll find a ton of protein alternatives here as well as tofu, like nut milks and beans to help boost your vivacity for the day. Not only does tofu provide a great source of protein, it also contains all nine essential amino acids and is a valuable source of iron which many of us are lacking. I hope the following recipes provide you with a little inspiration, as well as good food intentions to start the day right!

Starting
the day
right

PEAR AND PECAN BIRCHER MUESLI

SERVES 8

This is the perfect busy person's brekkie. If you know you need to make more effort with your diet in the mornings but can't see how you'd make the time (perhaps reluctant to set that alarm a little earlier?!) then this is the brekkie for YOU! Make it the night before to allow the flavours to soak in and the oats to soften, then all you need to do the next day is remember to get it out of the fridge. Soaking oats also means they retain more of their nutrients as it helps to decrease the amount of phytic acid (which prevents your body from absorbing the good stuff).

3 ripe pears

300g rolled oats

300ml almond or rice milk

100ml fresh apple or
   orange juice

2 tbsp maple syrup plus
   extra for drizzling

½ tsp mixed spice

100g mixed pumpkin and
   sunflower seeds

400g coconut milk yoghurt
   or soya milk yoghurt

60g pecans, roasted and
   chopped

Quarter, core and grate 2 of the pears into a large bowl. Add the oats, milk, juice, syrup, mixed spice and seeds and stir together. Cover and place in the fridge, overnight, to soak.

The following morning, quarter, core and slice the remaining pear. Stir the yoghurt into the muesli and serve in bowls with the sliced pear and pecans on top. Drizzle over a little more maple syrup, if desired.

QUINOA GRANOLA

SERVES 10–12

MAKES ABOUT 600G

I love granola but shop-bought can often be sugar laden and a stodgy way to start your day. This is so much lighter all round, easy to make and gives you a good shot of protein from the quinoa. Many people I come across still don't get quinoa, but once you start to use it in more versatile ways you'll see how much joy it can bring to a meal.

225g white or red quinoa

200g rolled oats

50g hemp seeds

50g pumpkin seeds

25g sunflower seeds

50g coconut oil, melted

5 tbsp maple syrup

½ tsp ground cinnamon

Pinch of sea salt

To serve
Non-dairy milk or yoghurt
Fruit

Preheat the oven to 180°C/160°C fan/350°F/gas mark 4 and line a baking tray with baking parchment.

Place all the ingredients in a large bowl and stir well to combine. Spread the mixture out, in an even layer, on the tray and bake for 20-25 minutes, stirring half way through, until golden and crispy. Remove and leave to cool completely.

Transfer to an airtight container and serve with your favourite non-dairy milk or yoghurt and fruit on top. It will keep for up to 2 weeks.

STRAWBERRY CHIA JAM

MAKES 2 X 250ML JARS

This versatile compote is the perfect little add-on for so many brekkies. Lob it on top of some coconut milk yoghurt, drizzle on to your morning porridge, or spread on toast or crackers if you're in a rush. It's full of mouth-watering strawberries for a hit of vitamins and contains no refined sugars so you won't suffer the inevitable sugar crash mid-morning. Make a batch and pop it in the fridge for whenever takes your fancy.

500g frozen strawberries
4 tbsp maple syrup
40g chia seeds

Put the strawberries and maple syrup into a pan and place over a medium-high heat. Cook for 15 minutes, stirring frequently, until the berries have collapsed down and the mixture has reduced and thickened slightly.

Stir in the chia seeds and continue cooking for another 3 minutes. Remove from the heat and leave to cool completely. Transfer into small sterilised jars and keep refrigerated for up to a week.

EASY SEEDED BREAD

MAKES 1 LOAF

Seeds are an important part of a vegan diet as they're a good protein alternative to animal products. This loaf is teeming with seeds so you can start your day right if you're a 'grab and go' kind of person who only has the time and inclination to spread a topping over some bread before leaving the house. Top slices of this seeded wonder bread with the Strawberry chia jam (page 17), your favourite nut butter or some spreadable coconut oil. If this is your first time making bread, get ready to make an easy, no-knead loaf.

300g wholegrain spelt flour
200g white spelt flour
3 tbsp poppy seeds
3 tbsp sesame seeds
3 tbsp sunflower seeds
1 tsp baking powder
1 tsp bicarbonate of soda
1 tsp sea salt
1 tbsp blackstrap molasses
  or maple syrup
540ml tepid water

Special equipment needed
900g loaf tin

Preheat the oven to 200°C/180°C fan/400°F/gas mark 6. Lightly grease the loaf tin and fully line with baking parchment.

Thoroughly mix all the dry ingredients together in a bowl, then add the blackstrap molasses or maple syrup and water and mix again until just combined.

Pour into the loaf tin and bake in the oven for 50 minutes, then carefully remove the loaf from its tin and continue to bake on a baking tray or the oven's wire rack for a further 10 minutes.

Remove the loaf from the oven and leave to cool completely before cutting, otherwise all the steam escapes resulting in a drier loaf. Once cool, cut into slices and enjoy spread with coconut oil and jam. It will keep in an airtight container for up to a week.

PARADISE PORRIDGE

SERVES 4

~~~~~~

On a cold, wet and classically British morning who doesn't want a bit of paradise in their lives? Porridge, although very good for us at the start of a day can be insanely boring so I'm on a constant morning mission to jazz my own bowl up. Oats are a great start to the day as they release energy slowly stopping us from having an energy spike then huge lull mid-morning. This flavoursome recipe is equally quick, easy, warming and comforting.

180g rolled oats

50g desiccated coconut

400ml tin coconut milk

1 tbsp coconut oil

To serve

Cacao nibs

Toasted coconut chips or
  extra desiccated coconut

Shake the tin of coconut milk to ensure the milk and solids have not separated. Then put the oats, desiccated coconut, most of the coconut milk and 260ml water in a medium pan and set over a medium heat. Simmer gently for 10 minutes, stirring now and again, until the porridge is thick and creamy. Stir in the coconut oil, until melted, then swirl through the remaining coconut milk.

Serve immediately, in bowls, with cacao nibs and toasted coconut chips or desiccated coconut scattered over.

BANANA PANCAKES

SERVES 4

Another fear for my family whenever I mention the V word is that they will miss out on their beloved pancakes. Luckily bananas easily act as an egg alternative in this recipe as they bind the mixture together so well. The flax gives a good fix of fibre and the vanilla a little added flavour. Top yours however you desire. I go for berries and coconut milk yoghurt but be as lavish as you like. Try nut butter mixed with maple syrup, Strawberry chia jam (page 17) or even the caramel sauce I use for my Date and almond cake (page 213).

2 large ripe bananas, peeled

90g white spelt flour or rice flour, sifted

80g ground flax seeds

2 tsp baking powder

300ml oat milk

1 tsp vanilla extract

¼ tsp sea salt

Coconut or sunflower oil, for frying

To serve
Mixed berries

Soya milk yoghurt or coconut milk yoghurt

Maple syrup

In a bowl mash one of the bananas and combine together with the flour, ground flax seeds, baking powder, milk, vanilla extract and salt, until smooth.

Put two teaspoons of oil in a large non-stick frying pan and set over a medium heat. Once hot, pour in a small ladleful of batter per pancake – you'll need to do this in batches, 2-3 at a time. Fry for 3 minutes until bubbles appear on the surface and the base is golden, then flip over and fry for another 2-3 minutes. Keep warm in a low oven while you cook the rest.

Slice the remaining banana. Divide the pancakes between your plates and top with the banana slices, berries, yoghurt and maple syrup. Serve immediately.

CASHEW, PEAR AND CHOCOLATE BAKED OATS

SERVES 4

This is a great winter warmer for cosy weekends when you have a little more time, or it's perfect served cold if you're organised and have made a batch the day before. Oats contain fibre which is good for your gut and can also improve blood sugar control. The pears and cashews add another needed boost of vitamins and protein to ensure you start your day right!

1 tbsp ground flax seeds

3 tbsp boiling water

200g rolled oats

1 tsp baking powder

1 tbsp cocoa powder plus extra for dusting

Pinch of sea salt

2 bananas, peeled

3 ripe pears, cored and thinly sliced

300ml cashew milk

4 tbsp cashews, roasted

3 tbsp cashew butter

Coconut milk yoghurt, to serve

Special equipment needed
18-20cm round or square casserole dish or cake tin

Preheat the oven to 200°C/180°C fan/400°F/gas mark 6. Grease the casserole dish or cake tin.

Place the ground flax seeds and water in a small bowl and set aside for at least 3 minutes. In another bowl combine the oats, baking powder, cocoa powder and salt.

Put the bananas, half the pears, milk and flax mixture into a blender and blitz until smooth. Pour into the dry mix and stir to thoroughly combine.

Pour half the oat mixture into the dish or tin, layer with half the remaining pear and cover with the rest of the oat mixture. Bake in the oven for 35-40 minutes until just set. Leave to cool, in the dish or tin, for 10 minutes.

To serve, spoon out into bowls and top with the remaining slices of pear, roasted cashews, cashew butter, a dollop of yoghurt and a little dusting of cocoa powder. It is also delicious served cold and will keep in the fridge for 2 days.

FRENCH TOAST WITH PEACHES AND CASHEW DRIZZLE

SERVES 4

My husband's one request for this book was for a vegan alternative to French toast. This is his absolute breakfast heaven and a total treat for those special occasions like birthdays or Christmas morning. It feels lavish and decadent and might appear impossible without eggs! But no, this recipe delivers on luxury and flavour with not an egg in sight! Jesse, this is for you . . .

2 tbsp chickpea (gram or besan) flour

350ml soya or oat milk

2 tbsp maple syrup plus extra for drizzling

2 tsp vanilla extract or paste

1 tsp ground cinnamon

8 thick slices of soft wholegrain or white bread

Coconut oil, for frying

To serve
Cashew butter

2 ripe peaches, stoned and cut into wedges

In a bowl, whisk together the flour, milk, maple syrup, vanilla and cinnamon until thoroughly combined, ensuring there are no lumps. Pour into a flat wide casserole dish. One by one lay each slice of bread into the mixture, for about 10-15 seconds on each side, so it is soft, but not falling apart.

Put one teaspoon of coconut oil into a large non-stick frying pan, set over a medium-high heat. Once hot, add two or three slices of bread and cook for 3-4 minutes on each side, until golden and slightly crispy. Cook the remaining bread in the same way, adding more coconut oil as needed. Serve the slices as and when they are ready or keep warm in a low oven.

Stack the hot French toast onto plates, drizzle over plenty of maple syrup and top with cashew butter and peach wedges. Serve immediately.

MISO SCRAMBLED TOFU AND AVOCADO ON RYE

SERVES 2

One of the reasons I find it hard to commit to being fully vegan is my love for eggs, so if I can find delicious substitutes then I'm happy. This recipe does just that as the scrambled tofu rivals the most buttery of scrambled eggs. The miso gives it so much flavour and the tofu offers up a lot of protein to keep you going all morning. There are a few recipes with miso in this book so if it's your first time using it don't worry about it going to waste, it is extremely versatile and gives flavour to many of my dishes in *Happy Vegan*.

400g firm tofu, drained

1 tbsp extra virgin olive oil plus extra for drizzling

2 garlic cloves, crushed

2cm piece of fresh ginger, peeled and grated

1 tbsp miso paste

200ml vegetable stock

2 slices of rye bread

1 avocado, halved, stoned and thinly sliced

2 spring onions, finely sliced

Sea salt and freshly ground black pepper

Tightly wrap the tofu in a clean tea towel. Over a sink, squeeze the tofu very firmly, tightening the tea towel as you go to extract as much water as possible, almost wringing out the tofu. Unwrap and crumble into a bowl, breaking up any larger pieces with a fork.

Heat the oil in a large non-stick frying pan over a medium-high heat. Add the tofu and stir-fry for 4-5 minutes until golden. Add the garlic and ginger and fry for another minute until aromatic. Combine together the miso paste and stock, add to the pan and cook for another 3-5 minutes, stirring now and again, until the stock has reduced and you are left with soft, scrambled tofu. Season to taste.

Meanwhile, toast the bread, drizzle with a little extra virgin olive oil and season. Top with the scrambled tofu and arrange the sliced avocado on the side. Scatter over the spring onions and serve immediately.

INDIAN SPICED POTATOES AND RAITA ON TOAST

SERVES 4

Eating a little bit of spice in the morning always makes me feel like I'm on holiday, so this recipe is great for weekends or days where there is no rush. The potatoes are easy to cook and should be enjoyed in a leisurely manner as every flavour dances across your taste buds. Spice up your life and bring the exotic into your life with these vegan darlings.

800g baby new potatoes

Olive oil, for frying

200g cherry tomatoes, halved

1 onion, chopped

3 tsp ground cumin

3 tsp ground coriander

1 tsp dried chilli flakes

5 garlic cloves, crushed

5 spring onions, finely sliced

Small handful of mint, leaves only, roughly chopped

200g soya milk yoghurt

4 slices of sourdough or white bread

2 avocados, halved, stoned and thinly sliced

Sea salt and freshly ground black pepper

Cook the potatoes in a large pan of boiling salted water for 15-20 minutes until tender. Drain thoroughly and cut into large bite-size pieces.

Coat the bottom of a large non-stick frying pan with olive oil and set over a high heat. Add the potatoes, tomatoes, onion and 2½ teaspoons each of the ground cumin and coriander and ½ teaspoon of the dried chilli flakes. Fry for about 12 minutes, flipping the potatoes every now and again, until golden and crispy in places. Reduce the heat, add most of the garlic and fry for another minute until aromatic. Remove from the heat and stir in the spring onions. Season to taste.

For the raita, mix together most of the mint and the yoghurt with the remaining garlic and spices, season to taste.

Toast the bread and top with the spiced potatoes, sliced avocado, raita and remaining mint leaves. Serve immediately.

SWEET POTATO ROSTIS

MAKES 6–8 ROSTIS

SERVES 2

~~~~~~

I love a rosti as they always look like they've taken lots of effort to make when they're actually as easy as can be! Vegetables aren't usually seen in the UK as something one would consume in the morning but if you're trying to up your fruit and veg intake it's a great way to squeeze some more in. Sweet potatoes are bursting with flavour, vitamins and fibre to promote gut health and general wellbeing.

1 large sweet potato, about 300g

1 tbsp miso paste

2 tsp tamari or soy sauce

1 tsp toasted sesame oil

½ tsp sesame seeds

1 tbsp white spelt flour

2 tbsp olive oil

100g coconut milk yoghurt

1 tsp ground cumin

1 tsp maple syrup

Small handful of flat leaf parsley, leaves only, roughly chopped

Sea salt and freshly ground black pepper

Peel and coarsely grate the sweet potato. Place the grated potato in the centre of a clean tea towel, fold over and press out as much liquid as possible. Transfer to a bowl and add the miso paste, tamari or soy sauce, sesame oil, sesame seeds and flour. Season with a pinch of salt and pepper and stir well to combine.

Heat the oil in a large non-stick frying pan, over a medium heat. Add 2 tablespoons of the sweet potato mixture to the pan and shape into a small round, repeat with the remaining mixture. Fry the rostis for 4-5 minutes until golden and crispy on one side, then gently flip over and fry for another 4-5 minutes, until golden and cooked through.

Combine the yoghurt, cumin and maple syrup together, and serve dolloped on the rostis with the parsley scattered over.

HOMEMADE BAKED BEANS

SERVES 6–8

You may think 'What is the point of making your own beans?' but once you've tasted these bad boys you'll be rushing for the tins of haricot beans. Knowing what has gone in to your food is extremely important as many of us are attempting to eradicate or at least limit the amount of processed foods we consume. These beans are a perfect example of a punchy, vegan, flavoursome alternative to shop-bought kinds. Plus, beans are one of the best protein alternatives for vegetarians and vegans and they're also a good source of fibre and B vitamins.

For the baked beans
3 tbsp extra virgin olive oil
2 onions, finely chopped
2 garlic cloves, crushed
2 tsp sweet smoked paprika
3 rosemary sprigs, leaved only, finely chopped
2 x 400g tins haricot beans, rinsed and drained
2 x 400g tins chopped tomatoes
3 tbsp maple syrup
2 tbsp soy sauce
1 tbsp Dijon mustard
2 tbsp red wine vinegar
Sea salt and freshly ground black pepper

To serve
Toasted sourdough or wholegrain bread
Sliced avocado (optional)
Tofu sausages (optional)

Place the oil in a medium pan, over a medium heat. Add the onions and sauté for 8-10 minutes until soft, but not coloured. Add the garlic, paprika and rosemary and fry for 2 minutes until aromatic. Add the remaining ingredients to the pan, stir well and bring to a boil. Immediately reduce the heat to low and simmer very gently for 30-40 minutes, stirring now and again, until thickened. Season generously with salt and pepper and a little more vinegar or maple syrup, to taste.

Serve the beans on toast, with some sliced avocado and/or tofu sausages, if liked. Keep any leftover beans in an airtight container, in the fridge, for up to 3 days or freeze them.

DATE AND TURMERIC SPICED BREAKFAST SMOOTHIE

SERVES 2

What a vibrant glass of goodness this is! You only have to look down the ingredients list to see the incredible nutrients you're about to consume with this start to the day. Dates which are an incredible source of natural sugar energy, spinach for iron, almond butter for protein and turmeric for a splash of colour and zingy flavour. Whizz it up, scoop it down and get going with your busy day.

1 banana, peeled, chopped and frozen

1 apple, cored and roughly chopped

100g spinach

4 Medjool dates, pitted

2 tbsp almond butter

350ml almond milk

4 tbsp ground hemp seeds

2 tsp vanilla extract

½ tsp ground turmeric

½ tsp mixed spice

Ice, to serve (optional)

Put the frozen banana in a food processor or blender and blitz until ground down. Add the rest of the ingredients and blitz for 1-2 minutes or until smooth.

Pour into two large glasses and serve immediately with ice, if you like.

BREAKFAST SMOOTHIE BOWLS

SERVES 2

On a family holiday a few years ago to Rio, we discovered the amazing local favourite of acai smoothie bowls. The locals eat them for breakfast or as a soothing snack, and we all quickly learned why. They have such a unique flavour which is a decadent concoction of berries with perhaps a touch of richness likened to chocolate.

As acai can be tricky to find in some supermarkets, either swap these for other berries or leave out altogether. The basic smoothie bowl is still delicious and packed with vitamins and nutrients that will set you up for the day, with iron in the greens, vitamin C in the fruit, and protein in the almond butter. You can also make these bowls looks extremely pretty if you're one of those types that likes to Instagram your food!

2 bananas, peeled and frozen

2 avocados, halved and stoned

80g spinach or 100g frozen acai berries

4 tbsp almond butter

120ml non-dairy milk

2 tsp vanilla extract

2 tbsp maple syrup

8 sprigs of mint, leaves only

Fruit, nuts and seeds of your choice, to serve

Place all the ingredients (choosing either spinach or acai berries) in a blender and blitz until completely smooth. Add a little more milk if you prefer a looser consistency.

Divide the mixture between two bowls and top with fruit, nuts and seeds of your choice. Serve immediately.

I wasn't given a middle name at birth but if I were to adopt one now it would be 'snacks'. Fearne Snacks Cotton. I'm the queen of snacks, the Goliath of grazing, I just cannot get enough. I'm not into eating huge portions at meal times, so instead prefer smaller meals with the opportunity for little bites in the in-between bits, to keep my energy up and my love affair with food ticking over.

Gone are the days when the word snack conjured up connotations of too salty crisps or an overly processed chocolate bar. As much as I loved snacking in the 80s, food choices have changed and luckily for the better. Snacks for me now means doing a bit of baking or cooking preparation and keeping the results in airtight containers in the kitchen cupboards for those slumps in the day where energy is low and the next meal time feels eons away. Vegan snacking is also pretty easy as there are so many ways to make this style of munching tasty and animal-product free.

This chapter features some very cool recipes I'm pretty excited about which should jazz up your train journey home after work, or enhance your break in-between jobs at home. I've also considered the sort of light bites you might want to have out on the kitchen counter when mates pop in for a cuppa and a good gossip. We constantly have people drifting in and out of the Cotton–Wood kitchen, so snacks are a necessity, especially at weekends. The Tahini and pomegranate fudge (page 49) feels particularly naughty and will surprise any friends or relatives confused by your choice to eat vegan. The Chocolate and strawberry chia squares (page 45) are a wonderful option to wrap up in a piece of foil when you know you have a busy day ahead. Knowing I've got one of these bad boys in the depths of my crammed handbag always puts a smile on my face when I'm rushing from meeting to meeting.

Get flicking through this chapter, get cooking and most importantly, GET SNACKING!

SNACKS

APRICOT AND RASPBERRY SLICES

SERVES 10–12 SLICES

These no-bake beauts mean no messing around but have maximum flavour and energy. The nuts and dried apricots give these slices a lot of vitamins and protein and also chewy enjoyment. There is definitely some magical alchemy at foot when raspberries and chocolate are combined as the flavours marry so perfectly together. Keep them in the fridge and enjoy them whenever you need a sweet pick me up.

300g unsulphured dried apricots

200g cashews

25g raw cacao powder or cocoa powder

1 tsp vanilla extract

3 tbsp chia seeds

Large pinch of salt

150g pecans

20g freeze dried raspberries, crushed

Special equipment needed
16 x 24cm cake tin

Line the cake tin fully with baking parchment and set aside.

Put the dried apricots, cashews, cacao powder or cocoa powder, vanilla extract, chia seeds and salt into a food processor and blitz for a few minutes, depending on the power of your machine, until the mixture comes together when pressed between your fingers.

Add the pecans and pulse a few times until roughly chopped. Transfer to the lined tin and smooth out with the back of a spoon.

Sprinkle the freeze dried raspberries over the mixture and gently press down, with the back of a spoon, to secure them into the surface.

Refrigerate for an hour, then cut into 10-12 slices. Keep in an airtight container for up to 3 days.

RASPBERRY AND LEMON SCONE CAKE

MAKES 8 WEDGES

As Brits it's in our DNA to like scones so a vegan option is a must. I wanted to give you a scone with a twist, hence the zingy lemon and tart raspberries. The flavours are so fresh and moreish and are perfect for a little afternoon tea with mates and a good cuppa. It's easy to make and doesn't need to look particularly neat. I like my scones a little rough around the edges!

350g wholegrain spelt flour plus extra for dusting

1 tsp baking powder

1 tsp bicarbonate of soda

60g coconut palm sugar

50g coconut oil, chilled and cut into small pieces

340ml oat milk

zest of 1 lemon and 2 tbsp lemon juice

200g frozen raspberries

To serve
Vegan margarine or coconut oil

Jam

Preheat the oven to 200°C/180°C fan/400°F/gas mark 6. Line a baking tray with baking parchment and dust it with flour.

Put the flour, baking powder, bicarbonate of soda, sugar and chilled coconut oil into a food processor and pulse on and off until it resembles fine breadcrumbs. Transfer to a large bowl.

Make a well in the centre of the dry ingredients and add the oat milk, lemon zest, lemon juice and raspberries. Gently combine the mixture together with a wooden spoon until you have a loose and shaggy dough. Don't be tempted to over mix it. With floured hands bring the dough together to form a rough ball.

Transfer the dough to the prepared tray and lightly flatten it into a 20-22cm round. Dust a long sharp knife with flour and cut the dough into 8 wedges of equal size but keep the wedges together in a round. Bake for 25-30 minutes until golden and firm to the touch.

Remove and leave to cool on the tray for 5 minutes, then gently transfer to a wire cooling rack to cool completely. Serve in wedges with vegan margarine or coconut oil, and jam to spread on top.

Any leftover wedges can be kept in an airtight container for up to 2 days or frozen for up to a month.

CHOCOLATE AND STRAWBERRY CHIA SQUARES

SERVES 16–20

My mouth is watering just thinking about these little jewels of joy. What a treat it is to remember around the 11am hunger pang that I have a stash of these tucked in a cake tin on my kitchen counter. The base is full of goodness and is refined sugar free and the chia jam and chocolate round off this sweet snack perfectly. Easy to make, impressive to show off and dreamy to scoff.

For the base

100g ground almonds

100g oat cakes

10 Medjool dates, pitted

60g coconut oil, melted

2 tbsp raw cacao or cocoa powder

Pinch of sea salt

For the filling

1 quantity strawberry chia jam (page 17)

For the topping

200g dark chocolate, minimum 70% cocoa solids, broken into small pieces

1 tbsp coconut oil

Special equipment needed

20 x 25cm cake tin

Line the tin fully with baking parchment.

Place all the base ingredients in a food processor and blitz until the mixture resembles fine crumbs and sticks together when pressed between your fingers. Firmly press the mixture into the lined tin. Place in the freezer for 10 minutes to set. Then spread the compote over the top in an even layer.

For the topping, place the chocolate and coconut oil in a heatproof bowl. Place the bowl over a pan of barely simmering water, ensuring the base of the bowl does not come into contact with the water. Stir now and again until the chocolate and coconut oil have melted and come together. Pour the chocolate over the compote layer and refrigerate for at least 1 hour until set.

Slice into squares and serve straight from the fridge.

NO BAKE CHOCOLATE PEANUT BUTTER COOKIES

MAKES 25

The words 'no bake' and 'cookie' are extremely appealing as it means we all get to eat them sooner! No waiting for them to cook and no staring at them as they cool to touch. The oats are a perfect fibre-packed base for these little treats and the nut butter is a great source of protein, making these cookies a delicious snack without the sugar crash later on down the line.

220g unsweetened smooth or crunchy peanut butter or other nut butter

2 tbsp coconut oil

170ml maple syrup

200g rolled oats

Pinch of sea salt

50g dark chocolate, minimum 70% cocoa solids

Line a tray with baking parchment.

Put the peanut butter, coconut oil and maple syrup in a large pan and set over a medium heat. Melt the mixture, stirring constantly, until fully combined. Turn up the heat and bring to a simmer, then immediately remove from the heat.

Stir in the oats and a pinch of salt until everything is evenly coated. Leave to cool for 10 minutes, then shape the mixture into 25 balls, about 1 tablespoon of mixture each, and gently flatten. Place on the lined tray, cover and refrigerate until set.

Break the chocolate into small pieces and place in a small heatproof bowl over a pan of barely simmering water, ensuring the base of the bowl does not come into contact with the water. Stir now and again until the chocolate has melted.

Drizzle the melted chocolate over the cookies and return the cookies to the fridge to allow the chocolate to set. Store in an airtight container, in the fridge, for up to a week.

TAHINI AND POMEGRANATE FUDGE

SERVES 8–10

You may think vegan sweet treats are no fun but wait until you get your chops around these delectable dreamboats. They're chewy, gooey and melt in your mouth and feel extremely creamy without any dairy ingredients. The pomegranate punch permeates the chewy fudge perfectly with the two complementary flavours marrying so well. Enjoy when you have that pang for a sweet moment.

100ml maple syrup

120g coconut palm sugar

60g coconut oil

340ml tahini

Pinch of sea salt

4 tbsp pomegranate seeds

Special equipment needed
16 x 24cm cake tin

Line the cake tin fully with baking parchment. Put the maple syrup and sugar into a pan over a medium-low heat and simmer gently until the sugar has mostly dissolved. Stir in the coconut oil, tahini and salt and mix until everything is completely combined.

Transfer the mixture to the lined tin and leave to cool for 10 minutes, then scatter over the pomegranate seeds, pressing them lightly into the mixture with the back of a spoon. Leave to cool completely then cover and refrigerate for 2 hours to set, or half an hour in the freezer. To serve, cut into small bite-size pieces. Store in an airtight container in the fridge for up to a week or frozen for up to a month.

ROSEMARY AND THYME SPICED NUTS

SERVES 4–6

If you find nuts boring or bland it is so easy to give them a spruce up with little fuss. These take minutes to make and are lovely served in a bowl when you have friends over or packed in a container to take for car journeys or pit stops at work.

200g cashews

200g pecans

200g almonds

3 tbsp fresh rosemary leaves, finely chopped

1 tbsp fresh thyme leaves

2 tsp sweet smoked paprika

3 tbsp olive oil

4 tbsp coconut palm sugar

2 tsp sea salt

Preheat the oven to 200°C/180°C fan/400°F/gas mark 6.

Place the nuts on a baking tray. Roast the nuts in the oven for 6-8 minutes, turning now and again, until a shade darker and aromatic. Take care not to let them burn.

Meanwhile, in a bowl combine together the rosemary, thyme, paprika, olive oil, sugar and salt. Pour over the hot roasted nuts and toss together until evenly coated. Leave to cool a little, then serve.

MULTI SEED CRACKERS

SERVES 2

Making your own vegan crackers might sound tricky – does the lack of egg mean they're going to crumble or be too brittle to pick up off the baking tray? Not at all! These are wonderfully robust and taste strangely buttery. I'm addicted to these little guys and make them at weekends ready for snacking on during the week ahead. Use them to dip into the Beetroot, tahini and chestnut dip (page 53), spread with a little almond butter or pack up to take on your travels and eat straight up!

90g white spelt flour plus extra for dusting

½ tsp baking powder

1 tbsp sesame seeds

1 tbsp chia seeds

1 tbsp poppy seeds

30g coconut oil, chilled and cut into small pieces

Sea salt

Preheat the oven to 180°C/160°C fan/350°F/gas mark 4. Line a baking tray with baking parchment.

Put the flour, baking powder, all the seeds, coconut oil and a large pinch of sea salt into a food processor and blitz until it resembles fine breadcrumbs. Transfer to a bowl and add 2 tablespoons of warm water, mix together until it forms a ball of dough, your hands are the best utensils for this. If the dough is crumbly, add a few drops of water at a time until it comes together into a smooth ball.

Roll out the dough as thinly as possible on a lightly floured surface, dusting with more flour as you go to prevent sticking. Brush the dough with a little water and sprinkle over a little more salt. Use a cookie cutter or cut the dough into odd shapes, squares and rectangles or anything you like. Transfer to the lined baking tray and bake for 12-14 minutes until dry and biscuity.

Remove from the oven and transfer to a wire cooling rack to cool completely. Store in an airtight container for up to a week and serve with any of the dips, see pages 53–6.

BEETROOT, TAHINI AND CHESTNUT DIP

SERVES 2

This is one of my favourite snacks and I usually have an airtight container of it stashed in the fridge. I love dolloping huge mounds of it on top of rice cakes or scooping it out with carrots for a double veggie hit. It's great to have out on the kitchen counter, if you have mates over, as it's not only delicious and nutritious but also has the most vibrant and beautiful colour.

200g cooked beetroot

50g cooked chestnuts

3 tbsp tahini

3 tbsp non-dairy yoghurt

½ tsp ground cumin

1 tbsp roughly chopped chives

Sea salt and freshly ground black pepper

Put all the ingredients, apart from the chives, into a food processor and blitz until almost smooth. Season to taste with salt and pepper and serve with the chives sprinkled over the top.

Serve with Multi seed crackers (page 52), pitta bread or vegetables to dunk into the dip.

SWEET POTATO WEDGES WITH CREAMY SPINACH DIP

SERVES 4

Silken tofu is such a favourite of mine, I love to use it in vegan dips, bakes and even desserts. It makes for a perfectly versatile base for flavours to work with and gives a wonderful consistency. It also offers protein and can help to reduce bad cholesterol levels. The sweet potato wedges are so comforting and packed with vitamin C. A lovely snack to dive in to with friends or family on a cold afternoon.

4 sweet potatoes, cut into wedges

2 tbsp olive oil

300g silken tofu

100g baby spinach

2 tbsp nutritional yeast

2 tsp miso paste

1 garlic clove

½ tsp ground cumin

Small handful of chives, roughly chopped

Sea salt and freshly ground black pepper

Preheat the oven to 200°C/180°C fan/400°F/gas mark 6.

Place the potato wedges on a baking tray. Drizzle over the oil and toss to coat. Season well and bake for 30 minutes, or until soft and golden.

Meanwhile, place the remaining ingredients, apart from the chives, into a blender with ¼ teaspoon of salt and blitz until smooth. Transfer to a bowl.

Serve the potato wedges with the chives scattered over and the spinach sauce on the side.

VEGAN CHEESY DIP

SERVES 4

For those cheese lovers wondering how they'll give up or limit the Cheddar and Brie get ready for a creamy vegan delight. The consistency is remarkably like the real thing and the flavour is moreish. The cashews provide the chance to consume a decent amount of protein and good fats, too.

This is perfect for dipping vegetables or nachos in and can also be dolloped on top of a vegan pizza. The cheese will firm up as it cools, so if you are not eating it immediately simply reheat for a brief time in the microwave or in a pan over a low heat, to soften.

80g cashews, chopped

200ml soya milk

2 tsp miso paste

1 tbsp nutritional yeast

4 tbsp tapioca flour

1 tsp garlic powder

¼ tsp sweet smoked paprika

2 tsp lemon juice

Sea salt and freshly ground black pepper

Cover the cashews in cold water and leave to soak overnight or cover them in boiling water and soak for 30 minutes.

Drain the nuts thoroughly and transfer to a blender or food processor with the remaining ingredients. Blitz until completely smooth. Transfer to a saucepan and set over a medium heat. Bring to simmering point while stirring all the time, cook for 6-8 minutes until thick and creamy. Remove from the heat, transfer to a bowl and leave to cool.

Serve with crackers or vegetables to dunk into the cheese, or on top of the Vegan nachos (opposite) or dollop onto Flatbread pizzas (page 120) or in sandwiches.

VEGAN NACHOS

SERVES 4

If I have mates over in between meal times I love to pop some snacks out, so we can chat and munch, and these always go down well. A perfect Sunday afternoon grazing option as the kids run around the kitchen and us shattered adults catch up on life. Once again featuring those all-important beans that are important in a vegan diet for protein and pack a lot of flavour for the taste buds.

200g tortilla chips

½ x 400g tin refried beans

150g Vegan cheesy dip (page 56) or shop-bought vegan cheese-style block

1 ripe avocado, halved, stoned and roughly chopped

2 tomatoes or 10 cherry tomatoes, roughly chopped

3 spring onions, finely sliced

3 pickled chillies, drained and thinly sliced

100g soya milk yoghurt

100g salsa

Handful of coriander, roughly chopped

Preheat the oven to 220°C/200°C fan/450°F/gas mark 8. Line a large baking tray with baking parchment.

Lay half the tortilla chips onto the lined tray and dollop over some of the refried beans and cheesy dip or crumble if using a cheese-style block. Repeat to use the remaining chips, beans and cheesy dip or block.

Bake in the oven for 15 minutes until the refried beans are soft and the dip or block has melted. Remove from the oven and spoon over the avocado, tomatoes, spring onions, chillies, yoghurt and salsa and scatter over the coriander.

Lunch is often the meal I find most difficult to keep vegan. If I am dashing around town and have little time to spare or am travelling in a part of the UK I'm less familiar with it can mean options are minimal. I have taken to making my own packed lunch for these very moments so I can still enjoy something bursting with flavour that will give me oodles of energy. I'll often pack an airtight container with Cauliflower rice salad with cannellini beans, avocado and radishes (page74) or Rice and veggie bowl (page 84), so I know I won't end up hungry and grumpy if shop-bought options are scarce.

Luckily my schedule is pretty varied, so now and then I'll find myself at home for lunchtime where I can knock something up in the kitchen only centimetres away from where I have been typing on my laptop. It's no surprise being this obsessed with food that I work from my kitchen counter even though there is a desk in the front room perfectly well suited to writing!

My daughter Honey is still home for lunch some days so it's nice to have a handful of quick and easy recipes that I can quickly knock up for us so we can eat together before she goes to nursery. A few of these vegan lunches she will share with me, others I'll try with her when she is a little older and more adventurous.

Jesse is sometimes home from work for lunch too and has been really enjoying a more plant-based diet recently. His favourite is The ultimate vegan sandwich (page 66). It's easy to pack this off for your lunch break at work or uni too. I'm a soup sister and would always opt for a bowl of something warm and comforting whatever the weather, so the Apple cider beetroot soup (page 64) has become a firm favourite of mine.

All these recipes are easy to knock up in the morning before you leave for a busy day, or at lunchtime if you're at home. I hope they inspire, tantalise and get your taste buds buzzing.

Lunch on the GO

WARM PEA, BROAD BEAN AND PINE NUT PASTA SALAD

SERVES 4

This pasta dish is so fresh and zingy. It feels like the perfect spring time lunch dish as its flavours remind me of being outside on a sunny day. It's so quick and easy to knock up in a rush but gives you so much more fun and flavour than a boring shop-bought sandwich.

80g pine nuts
400g fusilli pasta
200g frozen peas
150g frozen broad beans
Handful of mint, leaves only
3 garlic cloves
4 tbsp nutritional yeast
5 tbsp extra virgin olive oil
1 tsp dried chilli flakes
2 tbsp capers, rinsed
Zest of 1 lemon and 2 tbsp
   lemon juice
Salt and freshly ground
   black pepper

Preheat the oven to 200°C/180°C fan/400°F/gas mark 6.

Place the pine nuts on a baking tray and roast in the oven for 4-6 minutes, until a shade darker and aromatic. Watch them carefully as they burn very quickly. Remove and leave to cool.

Bring a large pan of salted water to the boil and cook the pasta for 7 minutes, then add the peas and broad beans and cook for another 3 minutes, until the pasta is al dente. Drain the pasta and vegetables, reserving a cup of the cooking water. Peel the outer skin of the broad beans, if you like, and return the pasta and beans to the pan.

While the pasta is cooking, put three-quarters of the pine nuts and three-quarters of the mint leaves into a food processor with the garlic, nutritional yeast and olive oil. Blitz to a rough paste and season generously, to taste.

Add the pine nut mixture into the pasta with the chilli flakes, capers, lemon zest and juice and a few tablespoons of the pasta cooking water, to create a sauce. Gently stir to combine. Taste and adjust the seasoning if necessary.

Divide the pasta and sauce between bowls and serve with the remaining pine nuts and mint scattered over.

APPLE CIDER BEETROOT SOUP

SERVES 4

I'm a massive soup fan. I make at least one variety each week as it's such a handy meal to have stored in a container in the fridge or even frozen for later on down the line. Fortunately my kids also like soup, if blended well, so I can ensure they're getting some good old veggies in their diet. Beetroots give so much flavour and make the perfect base for soup. Apple cider vinegar is good for the tummy, especially if unsettled, so it's nice to be able to incorporate it into our meals.

850g beetroot, peeled and
   roughly chopped
3 tbsp olive oil
600ml vegetable stock
200ml coconut milk
1-2 tbsp apple cider vinegar
Sea salt and freshly ground
   black pepper

To serve
Coconut milk yoghurt
Small bunch of dill,
   chopped

Preheat the oven to 200°C/180°C fan/400°F/gas mark 6.

Place the beetroot in a roasting tin, drizzle the oil over, toss to coat and season well. Cover with foil and roast for 35-40 minutes until completely tender.

When the beetroot is almost cooked, warm the stock and coconut milk in a pan over a low heat, just until combined. Place the beetroot and stock mixture in a blender or food processor and blitz until completely smooth. Season to taste, bearing in mind some vegetable stocks are already salted. Add in 1 or 2 tablespoons of the apple cider vinegar, according to your taste. You may find the soup needs a little more salt once the vinegar is added.

Serve in bowls with a dollop of coconut yoghurt on top and the dill scattered over.

THE ULTIMATE VEGAN SANDWICH

SERVES 2

Some might feel a little stuck when asked to prepare a vegan sandwich as we are almost indoctrinated that a sarnie needs to be jammed with meat, egg or cheese, but this lunch on the go will prove otherwise. It's hearty, filling and boasts a lot of goodness to boot. The tofu offering up protein and flavour, the hummus and avocado giving us some good fats and the garlic and mustard adding a wallop of flavour.

6 tbsp hummus

2 tsp white miso paste

2 tsp Dijon mustard

Large handful of salad cress

1 carrot, grated

1 beetroot, grated

2 tsp balsamic vinegar

2 tbsp extra virgin olive oil

200g smoked tofu, drained and sliced

1 avocado, halved, stoned and sliced

1 small garlic clove, crushed

4 slices of wholegrain bread

Sea salt and freshly ground black pepper

In a bowl, combine together the hummus, miso paste and mustard. Set aside.

In another bowl, combine together the cress, carrot, beetroot, balsamic vinegar and 1 tablespoon of the olive oil. Season well.

Heat 1 tsp of the remaining olive oil in a non-stick frying pan and fry the tofu slices until golden. Remove and season.

Mash the avocado with the garlic and the remaining 2 teaspoons of olive oil and season.

To assemble, slather some of the hummus mixture over 2 slices of the bread and top with the vegetable mix, tofu and avocado. Spread the remaining hummus mixture over the remaining slices of bread and place on top of the filling, hummus side down. Cut in half and serve immediately.

CHINESE-STYLE TOFU, CUCUMBER AND CASHEW SALAD

SERVES 4

Salads can be seen as a little dull but this beautiful and zingy salad is hearty and filling as well as delicious. It's so quick to make and ensures that vegans are getting a plentiful amount of protein with the nuts and tofu. Cashews seem to release even more flavour when roasted so there's a lovely rich taste to this dish.

50g cashews

5 spring onions, finely sliced

2cm piece of fresh ginger, peeled and grated

2 garlic cloves, crushed

1 tsp chilli oil, or more to taste

2 tbsp tahini

1½ tbsp maple syrup

1½ tbsp toasted sesame oil

2 tbsp soy sauce

2 tbsp rice vinegar

400g firm tofu, drained, pressed and cut into 1cm cubes

1 cucumber

100g lamb's lettuce

1 tsp dried chilli flakes, to serve (optional)

Preheat the oven to 200°C/180°C fan/400°F/gas mark 6.

Place the nuts on a baking tray. Roast the cashews in the oven for 5-6 minutes until a shade darker and aromatic. Remove and leave to cool.

Place three-quarters of the sliced spring onions in a bowl with the ginger, garlic, chilli oil, tahini, maple syrup, sesame oil, soy sauce and rice vinegar. Whisk to combine and add more chilli oil, to taste, if liked.

Place the tofu cubes in a bowl and pour over half the dressing. Gently stir to combine and set aside for 15 minutes to marinate.

Meanwhile, half the cucumber lengthways and scoop out the seeds with the tip of a teaspoon. Cut into thick slices on an angle and add to the bowl of tofu with the remaining dressing. Lightly bash up or coarsely chop the cashews so they are not whole. Add most of them to the bowl and stir to combine.

Arrange the lettuce on a large platter and spoon over the marinated tofu, cucumber and dressing. Scatter over the dried chilli flakes, remaining spring onions and cashews and serve immediately.

CARROT, CUMIN AND COCONUT SOUP

SERVES 4

The flavours in this soup will blow your mind. They're comforting, dreamy and work so well together. The coconut milk makes it very creamy and moreish and the cumin seeds take the flavour to a whole new level. I love making up a big batch of this soup and then storing it in the fridge for another day or even freezing it – it freezes well for a couple of months.

4 tbsp olive oil

2 tbsp coconut oil

2 onions, finely chopped

3 garlic cloves, crushed

1 tbsp cumin seeds

500g carrots, roughly chopped

400ml vegetable stock

400ml tin coconut milk

Sea salt and freshly ground black pepper

Coconut milk yoghurt, to serve

Put 1 tablespoon of the olive oil into a large pan together with the coconut oil, onions, garlic and 2 teaspoons of the cumin seeds. Set over a medium heat and sauté for 8 minutes, stirring frequently, until the onions are translucent and soft. Take care not to let them brown.

Add the carrots, stock and coconut milk and bring to a boil. Reduce the heat and simmer for 30 minutes until slightly reduced and the carrots are tender. Leave to cool for a few minutes, then transfer to a blender and blitz until completely smooth. Season to taste with salt and pepper.

Put the remaining olive oil and cumin seeds into a small pan over a medium-high heat and fry for 1-2 minutes, just until the cumin seeds begin to sizzle and become fragrant. Season with a little salt and pepper.

Serve the soup in bowls topped with a dollop of the coconut yoghurt and the cumin oil drizzled over.

QUINOA NORI ROLLS

SERVES 4

Making nori rolls is a real fave for me and my step-daughter Lola. There is something so therapeutic about the process of making them and if you've never dabbled with homemade sushi it's really rather easy! The quinoa makes a nice change from rice for an added dose of protein alongside the tofu and the avocado ensures we get some good fats to promote healthy skin and nails. A joyful roll of goodness.

200g quinoa, rinsed

2 tbsp rice vinegar

1 tbsp mirin

6 nori sheets, halved

1 avocado, halved, stoned and thinly sliced

60g baby spinach

1 red pepper, deseeded and thinly sliced

200g smoked tofu, drained and cut into thin matchsticks

For the miso sauce

2 tbsp miso paste

Juice of 1 lime

2 tsp maple syrup

1 tsp soy sauce

2cm piece of fresh ginger, peeled and grated

Place the quinoa in a lidded pan with 500ml water. Bring to a boil, then reduce the heat to low, cover with the lid and cook for 12-15 minutes or until all the water has been absorbed. Turn off the heat, stir in the rice vinegar and mirin and spread out on a tray to cool.

Meanwhile, for the sauce, combine all the ingredients together in a bowl and set aside.

When the quinoa is cool, take one half sheet of nori and place on a board, shiny side down. Place 2½ tablespoons of quinoa about 3cm in from the bottom corner of the nori, and position it on an angle, so it is easy to roll into a cone shape. Place a little avocado, spinach, red pepper and tofu on top, then gently roll up the nori sheet, starting at the end you placed the quinoa on, until you have a cone shape. Use a little piece of the cooked quinoa to stick the outside edge of the nori sheet to the inner cone, so it stays in place. Carefully move to a plate and repeat with the remaining ingredients, to make 12 cones in total.

Serve the cones with the miso sauce drizzled over, or just dunk the cones in the sauce as you eat.

CAULIFLOWER RICE SALAD WITH CANNELLINI BEANS, AVOCADO AND RADISHES

SERVES 4

I'm a huge fan of cauliflower 'rice'. I love that we can replace a white carb with some extra veg in our diets without much effort. It's so quick and easy to prepare and cook too. If you don't have a food processor you can easily grate your cauli florets to mimic rice too. The mustard makes a huge flavoursome impact in this dish and the beans give a dose of protein that we all need half way through our day to help keep us feeling full.

500g cauliflower florets

8 tbsp olive oil

3 garlic cloves, crushed

1 tsp ground cumin

1 tsp sweet smoked paprika

4 tbsp balsamic vinegar

1 tsp Dijon mustard

1 tsp maple syrup

1 avocado, halved, stoned and thinly sliced

80g rocket

400g tin cannellini beans, drained and rinsed

10 radishes, finely sliced

4 tbsp hummus

2 tbsp pumpkin seeds

Sea salt and freshly ground black pepper

Put the cauliflower florets into a food processor and pulse until it resembles grains of rice. Add 2 tablespoons of the oil to a large non-stick pan and set over a medium heat. Add the garlic and sauté for 2 minutes until aromatic. Add the cauliflower, cumin and paprika and fry for about 6 minutes, stirring frequently, until tender. Season to taste.

Put the remaining olive oil, balsamic vinegar, Dijon mustard and maple syrup into a jug and whisk until it comes together into a smooth dressing. Season to taste.

Divide the cauliflower rice between bowls and top with the avocado, rocket, cannellini beans, radishes and hummus. Drizzle over the dressing, to taste, and scatter over the pumpkin seeds. Serve immediately.

MISO BUTTER BEANS WITH QUINOA

SERVES 4–6

There are so many beans to choose from when considering how to incorporate this vital source of protein into a vegan diet. Butter beans are one of my faves as they taste delicious without much work and can be added to so many recipes with ease. The creamy miso flavouring really works with the beans in this light lunch, as well as the rich tahini. One of my favourites to knock up when I'm at home for lunch.

300g quinoa, rinsed

3 tbsp olive oil

Large handful of flat leaf parsley, leaves only, roughly chopped

1 onion, finely chopped

3 garlic cloves, crushed

3cm piece of fresh ginger, peeled and grated

½ tsp ground turmeric (optional)

2 tbsp miso paste

500ml vegetable stock

2 x 400g tins butter beans, rinsed and drained

2 tbsp tahini

1 tbsp pomegranate molasses or balsamic vinegar

50g baby spinach

50g rocket

Sea salt and freshly ground black pepper

Place the quinoa in a lidded pan with 600ml water and a pinch of salt. Bring to a boil, then reduce the heat to low, cover with the lid and cook for 12-15 minutes or until all the water has been absorbed. Turn off the heat, stir in 1 tablespoon of the olive oil and most of the parsley. Leave to one side.

Heat the remaining oil in a pan. Add the onion and sauté for 8 minutes over a medium heat. Add the garlic, ginger, turmeric and a large pinch of salt and pepper and fry for another minute or two until fragrant.

Add the miso, stock and butter beans and bring to a boil. Reduce the heat and simmer for 15 minutes until the liquid has reduced a little. Stir in the tahini and pomegranate molasses or vinegar and season to taste. Fold in the spinach and rocket.

Serve the quinoa in bowls topped with the miso butter beans and greens and the remaining parsley.

FLATBREADS WITH HUMMUS, SUNDRIED TOMATOES AND OLIVES

SERVES 6

Whilst on *Saturday Kitchen*, as a guest, I saw the remarkable cook Sabrina Ghayour whip up flatbreads in record time. I've always been a bit scared to make bread as it seems so technical and precarious but these vegan flatbreads are so easy to make and always impressive to serve up to mates.

200g white spelt flour plus extra for dusting

½ tsp fine sea salt

2 tbsp extra virgin olive oil

To serve

Hummus

Sundried tomatoes

Small handful of flat leaf parsley, leaves only, roughly chopped

Black olives

Extra virgin olive oil

Sweet smoked paprika

In a large bowl combine the flour and salt together. Add the oil and 5 tablespoons of water and bring together into a dough. Gradually add a further 2 tablespoons of water to form a smooth and soft dough. It should not be sticky. Knead for 2 minutes just to make sure everything is well combined. Cover and set aside for 15 minutes to rest.

Divide the dough into 6 equal pieces and roll each piece into a ball. Dust your work surface with flour and roll each ball out into a thin round measuring about 22cm. Dust with flour as you go to ensure the dough doesn't stick.

Place a large non-stick frying pan over a low-medium heat, add a flatbread and cook for about 1 minute on each side until just cooked through. Remove to a plate and immediately cover with a clean tea towel. Repeat to cook the remaining breads.

To serve, place a warm flatbread on a plate and dollop the hummus on top, then scatter over the sundried tomatoes, parsley and olives. Drizzle over some extra virgin olive oil and dust with a little smoked paprika.

The flatbreads freeze well. Allow to cool completely then layer the bread with baking parchment between each one and wrap in foil. When you're ready to eat them, simply pop in the toaster.

TOMATO DAHL
WITH FLATBREADS

SERVES 4

Dahl is a really good vegan option for a quick lunch as it is predominantly lentils which are a good source of magnesium, fibre and complex carbohydrates that help to boost the metabolism. Never underestimate a lentil! This is also very much a 'chuck it in the pan' job so little fuss for an amazing meal all round. Serve with the flatbreads (page 79) or straight up or with rice.

260g red split lentils, washed

4 garlic cloves, crushed

2 tbsp soy sauce

2 tsp mild curry powder

1 tsp miso paste

400 tin chopped tomatoes

400g tin coconut milk

4 tbsp soya milk yoghurt or coconut milk yoghurt plus extra to serve

4 homemade flatbreads (page 79) or shop-bought flatbreads

Small handful of flat leaf parsley, leaves only, roughly chopped

Sea salt and freshly ground black pepper

Extra virgin olive oil, to serve

Put the lentils into a pan with the garlic, soy sauce, curry powder, miso paste, chopped tomatoes and coconut milk. Bring to a boil, then reduce the heat and simmer for 15 minutes, stirring frequently to stop the lentils sticking to the base of the pan. Add the yoghurt and simmer for another 5 minutes until you have a creamy dahl. Season to taste.

When the dahl is cooked, warm the flatbreads in a toaster or oven and serve with the lentils, topped with extra yoghurt, chopped parsley and a drizzle of olive oil.

RUNNER BEANS WITH RED ONION, RED PEPPER AND TOMATO SAUCE

SERVES 4

A little leftovers experiment one weekend led me to this vegan lunch on-the-go recipe. I often forget to buy runner beans or ignore them on the supermarket shelf, but this recipe reminded me how versatile and flavoursome they can be. Easy to make and tasty, serve straight up, on top of pasta or even on bread as an open sandwich, such as dark rye.

½ red onion, roughly chopped

1 red pepper, deseeded and roughly chopped

150g cherry tomatoes

3 garlic cloves

2 tbsp balsamic vinegar

1 tbsp extra virgin olive oil plus extra to serve

400g runner beans, cut in half on the diagonal

Small handful of flat leaf parsley, leaves only, roughly chopped

Sea salt and freshly ground black pepper

Preheat the oven to 200°C/180°C fan/400°F/gas mark 6.

Put the red onion, red pepper, cherry tomatoes and garlic into a roasting tin. Drizzle over the vinegar and olive oil and season well. Roast for 25 minutes, stirring half way through, until the vegetables have softened and slightly charred. Transfer into a food processor or blender and blitz into a rough sauce.

Meanwhile, add the runner beans to a large pan of boiling salted water. Simmer for 3-4 minutes, until tender, but not limp. Drain well.

Transfer the beans to a large serving dish, dollop over the vegetable sauce, drizzle over some more extra virgin olive oil and scatter over the parsley. Serve immediately.

RICE AND VEGGIE BOWL

SERVES 4

I can never quite judge the amount of rice or pasta I make so there is usually some left over – perfect for this recipe. Do make sure you follow these guidelines – cooked rice needs to be cooled to room temperature within an hour of cooking, so remove it from the pan and spread it out in a shallow airtight container. Once cool pop a lid on and chill in the fridge for up to 2 days. Only reheat rice ONCE, never twice.

For the dressing
3cm piece of fresh ginger, peeled and grated

2 garlic cloves, crushed

2 tbsp white miso paste

2 tbsp soy sauce

2 tbsp toasted sesame oil

1 tbsp sesame seeds

For the rice and vegetables
450g cooked brown rice

400g tin kidney beans, rinsed and drained

2 sweet potatoes, unpeeled and cut into 2cm cubes

1 tbsp coconut oil

60g kale, stalks removed and roughly chopped

400g smoked tofu, drained and cut into 2cm cubes

3 spring onions, finely sliced

Sea salt and freshly ground black pepper

For the dressing, dry fry the sesame seeds in a small pan for 3-5 minutes, then put all the ingredients into a jug with 1 tablespoon of water and whisk until thoroughly combined.

Place the rice in a large bowl and stir in 2 tablespoons of the dressing. Set aside. Place the beans in a dry pan and set over a medium heat, stirring gently. Once hot transfer to a bowl with 1 tablespoon of the dressing and stir to combine.

Bring a small pan of salted water to the boil and cook the sweet potato chunks for 4 minutes. Drain thoroughly. Heat the coconut oil in a large non-stick frying pan over a high heat and add the sweet potato. Fry for 6 minutes, stirring now and again, until golden and cooked through. Season to taste, remove the potatoes from the pan and set aside.

Place the frying pan back over the high heat, add 1 tablespoon of water and the kale. Stir fry for 5 minutes until tender and vibrant green. Transfer the kale to a bowl and stir in 1 tablespoon of the dressing.

Add the tofu to the pan and fry over a high heat for 3 minutes. Season well and set aside in a bowl.

When ready to serve, heat the rice in the pan or the microwave until piping hot (around 2-3 minutes at full power in the microwave) and divide equally between 4 bowls. Top each bowl with a quarter of the kidney beans, sweet potato, kale and tofu and pour over the remaining dressing. Scatter over the spring onions. Serve immediately.

PEPPER, AVOCADO, BLACK BEAN AND RICE BURRITOS

SERVES 4

When I was pregnant with my first-born I pretty much survived solely on burritos. The craving was insatiable as I had a need for multiple flavours and a meal that I could fold into my mouth at break neck speed. My love of the burrito has remained all these years later, so it was a lot of fun creating a vegan option for those wanting to ditch the cheese. It's easy enough to make either to eat at home or for a packed lunch – simply wrap in parchment paper and pop in an airtight container. A great lunch you can quite literally eat on the go.

1 tbsp olive oil

2 red peppers, deseeded and chopped

½ x 400g tin black beans, drained and rinsed

2 garlic cloves, crushed

1 tsp ground cumin

½ tsp sweet smoked paprika

100g cooked brown rice

2 wholegrain tortillas or gluten-free tortillas

1 baby gem lettuce, roughly chopped

1 avocado, halved, stoned and sliced

To serve
Small handful of parsley or coriander leaves, roughly chopped

Non-diary yoghurt

1 lime, cut into wedges

Sea salt and freshly ground black pepper

Heat the olive oil in a medium pan over a high heat, add the red pepper and fry for 5 minutes, until slightly charred and beginning to soften. Reduce the heat, add the black beans, garlic, cumin, paprika and season well. Fry for another 3 minutes.

When ready to serve, place a large non-stick frying pan over a high heat. Warm the rice until piping hot (you can also use a microwave to do this, around 2-3 minutes on full power) and set aside in a bowl. Use the pan to then heat the tortillas for about 30 seconds on each side or until softened.

To assemble the burritos, transfer the tortillas to two plates and divide the rice, lettuce, avocado, red pepper and black bean mixture between them. Scatter over some parsley or coriander, dollop a little yoghurt on top and season to taste. Fold over the edges of the tortillas to enclose the filling. Serve the lime wedges on the side to squeeze over.

It is unrealistic to think that any of us can cook every single meal from scratch. As if we have the time to mooch about playing music, whilst a slow-cook casserole simmers away in the hazy background of our lunchtimes. Life gets in the way. There will be days where we do order that cheeky takeaway and evenings where we're so tired a bowl of porridge is the only thing we can be bothered to cook up (I actually quite like a bowl of porridge for dinner, don't judge!) – and lunchtime can be the hardest time for this.

Yet there are also those glorious weekends where we can plan, prep and then savour every part of the process of cooking and eating lunch. Long and lazy is almost a luxury in this fast-paced world today but something we must make time for when we can.

For me, Sundays, in particular, become a day designed for PJ wearing, buoyant feel-good music and a lot of food. I have a specific playlist that I whack on loud, my hair will be piled on my head in a messy bun and no doubt the kids will be charging around me or kicking a football through the kitchen. Brilliant chaos but at the heart of it always lies food. My kids often get involved and help stir what's on the hob or sit on the counter watching me whilst we chat. These are moments I cherish and enjoy more than anything. Give me a home cooked meal made with love over a fancy restaurant any day. Lunches for famished family members, early dinners for friends with young kids, or hearty meals for my stepchildren after sports matches and muddy falls. I love being a hostess and putting delicious, nutritious food on plates for people I love. No better feeling.

These dishes feature a lot of lentils, legumes and colourful veg to ensure that you're getting all the vitamins and protein needed if you are to commit to a vegan diet. There are also some dishes that feature tofu as it's one of my go-to ingredients for protein and amino acids. These long and lazy meals will leave you feeling comfortably full and ready to rumble. Whether it's Mac and cashew cheese (page 99) for those needing some comfort and nostalgia or the Squash, lentil, mushroom and thyme casserole (page 109) for a big help-yourself-out-of-the-pot affair, I'm happy to go 'long and lazy' whenever I can.

LONG AND LAZY

TOMATO, PESTO AND LENTIL BAKED PEPPERS

SERVES 4

For all dahl lovers out there, this dish is for you. The creamy lentils combined with the juicy peppers is a real taste sensation and the vegan pesto gives a wonderfully nutty and decadent finish to this meal. I love stuffed peppers as they feel like a bit of a treat. I think I nostalgically link them back to childhood meals out when they were seen as a bit posh! Give this favourite a go and enjoy every mouthful.

4 red peppers, halved lengthways and deseeded

1 tbsp olive oil

200g red split lentils, washed

200g baby plum tomatoes, halved

4 garlic cloves crushed

2 tbsp soy sauce

1 tsp ground coriander

1 tsp ground cumin

3 tbsp coconut milk yoghurt

4 tbsp vegan pesto

Small handful of chives, roughly chopped

4 tbsp flaked almonds, roasted

Sea salt and freshly ground black pepper

Preheat the oven to 200°C/180°C fan/400°F/gas mark 6. Line a baking tray with baking parchment.

Put the peppers onto the lined baking tray and drizzle the olive oil over. Season well with salt and pepper and roast for 20 minutes, or until beginning to soften, but still holding their shape.

Place the lentils in a pan with the tomatoes, garlic, soy sauce, ground coriander and cumin and cover with 400ml water. Bring to a boil, reduce the heat and simmer gently for 15 minutes, stirring frequently to stop the lentils sticking to the base of the pan. Add the yoghurt and simmer for another 5 minutes.

Spoon the lentils into the pepper halves and return to the oven for 10 minutes. Remove, dollop the pesto on top and scatter over the chives and flaked almonds. Serve immediately.

BEETROOT FALAFEL

SERVES 4

Falafels can be bought in most supermarkets these days and they do make a brilliant, hearty vegan option, but I always think homemade ones taste so much better and are also pretty fun to make. Chickpeas are of course a great source of fibre which aids healthy digestion and also boasts a lot of protein, making them perfect for a vegan lifestyle. The beetroots give another dose of vitamins and vibrant colour to these little balls of fun. Pop them in a wrap with some salad and hummus or enjoy on top of a salad or flatbread.

1½ x 400g tins chickpeas, drained and rinsed

1 carrot, grated

2 cooked beetroot, grated

2 garlic cloves, crushed

1 tsp ground cumin

1 tsp ground coriander

60g rice flour or spelt flour

Small handful of flat leaf parsley, leaves only, roughly chopped

Sunflower oil, for frying

Sea salt and freshly ground black pepper

To serve
Hummus

Green leaves

Homemade flatbreads (page 79) or shop bought flatbreads (optional)

Put the chickpeas into a food processor and pulse on and off until they are finely chopped. Add the carrot, beetroot, 1 teaspoon of salt and a grinding of pepper and pulse again until everything is roughly chopped. Transfer to a large bowl.

Mix in the garlic, cumin, coriander, flour and most of the parsley and squeeze with your hand so it holds together. Roll the mixture into 16 balls of equal size, about 1½ tablespoons of mixture per falafel. Slightly flatten each ball with your hands, so they will sit flat in a pan.

Cover the base of a medium non-stick frying pan with 5mm of sunflower oil and place over a medium-high heat. Once the oil is hot, add the falafels and fry on each side for 4-5 minutes until golden brown, slightly crispy and cooked through. Remove and drain on kitchen paper then keep warm in a low oven.

Serve as a salad with hummus and green leaves, or with flatbreads, if liked, and the remaining parsley scattered on top.

PIRI PIRI TOFU

SERVES 4

I adore this dish as it's so flavoursome, tangy and massively comforting. It's pretty easy to knock up as most of the ingredients are simply whizzed in a blender or food processor, yet it tastes so sophisticated. It's bursting with protein from the tofu and if you team it with brown rice it will keep your energy levels up, stopping you feeling sluggish. Peri Peri perfect.

For the piri piri sauce
4 garlic cloves, peeled
1 roasted red pepper, from a jar, drained
½ red onion, roughly chopped
1 tbsp extra virgin olive oil
3 tbsp lemon juice
2 tsp maple syrup
2-4 red chillies, deseeded
Sea salt and freshly ground black pepper

For the tofu and vegetables
400g smoked tofu, drained and cut into 2cm cubes
400g tin kidney beans, drained and rinsed
200ml vegetable stock
300g broccoli, chopped into bite-sized florets
Large handful of flat leaf parsley, leaves only, roughly chopped
1 red chilli, deseeded and thinly sliced

To serve
Rice
Lime wedges

To make the sauce, put all the ingredients into a blender or food processor, adding 2 chillies to start with, and blitz until you have a mostly smooth sauce. Season to taste and add more chillies, one at a time, if liked.

Put the sauce, tofu cubes, beans, stock and broccoli florets into a large pan and bring to a rolling boil for 2 minutes. Reduce the heat a little and simmer for 10 minutes. Taste and adjust the seasoning.

Divide the tofu and sauce between plates and scatter over the parsley and chilli. Serve with rice and lime wedges, on the side, to squeeze over.

CHINESE-STYLE DUMPLINGS

SERVES 4–6

My dear friend Gok Wan came over to my house for Chinese New Year celebrations this year and gave me a master class in how to make beautiful handmade dumplings. I just had to include a vegan dumpling option in this book as they've become one of my favourite dishes to make.

200g firm tofu, drained

3 tbsp sunflower oil

½ courgette, finely chopped

100g shitake mushrooms, finely chopped

3cm piece of fresh ginger, peeled and grated

3 garlic cloves, crushed

2 spring onions, finely chopped

2 tbsp soy sauce

1 tbsp toasted sesame oil

30-35 white round dumpling skins (available online or from Asian supermarkets)

1 tbsp chives, roughly chopped

Sea salt and freshly ground black pepper

For the dipping sauce
5 tbsp soy sauce

1½ tbsp rice vinegar

Pinch of dried chilli flakes

Tightly wrap a clean tea towel around the tofu. Over a sink, squeeze the tofu very firmly, tightening the tea towel as you go to extract as much water as possible. Crumble the tofu into a bowl.

Heat 1 tablespoon of the sunflower oil in a large non-stick frying pan over a medium-high heat. Add the tofu, courgette, mushrooms, ginger, garlic, spring onions, soy sauce and sesame oil. Stir-fry until mostly dry – around 6-10 minutes. Season to taste then transfer to a food processor and blitz on and off until finely ground, taking care not to process it into a paste.

Place a dumpling skin in your palm and place 1 teaspoon of mixture in the centre. Brush the edge with a little water, then fold the skin around the filling, so the outer edges meet. You can pleat the edges together too (follow an online video tutorial if you are unsure!).

Put 1 tablespoon of the remaining oil into a frying pan with a lid and set over a medium heat. Once hot, add as many dumplings as your pan allows, taking care not to over crowd the pan. Fry for 3-4 minutes until the bases are golden, then add 3 tablespoons of water and place the lid on top to steam the dumplings for 3 minutes. Remove the lid, and fry for another 2-3 minutes until cooked through and golden and crispy on the base. Remove from the pan and transfer to a plate. Cook the remaining dumplings in the same way.

For the sauce, combine all the ingredients together. Serve the dumplings with the chives sprinkled over and the dipping sauce.

MAC AND CASHEW CHEESE

SERVES 4

Is there anything greater than Mac 'n' cheese? The creamy, comforting and warming qualities of this dish will ensure it remains a firm favourite classic of mine forever. Making vegan cheese has been a real revolution for me lately. I LOVE cheese so trying to reduce my dairy intake has been something I've taken care and time to explore throughout this journey. Cashews make such a brilliant base for all things 'vegan cheesy' and the nutritional yeast gives it real flavour.

100g cashews, roughly chopped

350g macaroni

220ml soya milk

1 tbsp miso paste

2 tbsp nutritional yeast

5 garlic cloves, crushed

1½ tbsp Dijon mustard

2 tsp lemon juice

30g fresh breadcrumbs

Small handful of flat leaf parsley, leaves only, very finely chopped

¼ tsp sweet smoked paprika

3 tbsp olive oil

Sea salt and freshly ground black pepper

Cover the chopped cashews in boiling water and soak for 30 minutes. While the nuts are soaking, bring a large pan of salted water to the boil and cook the macaroni, according to the packet instructions. Drain and set aside.

Preheat the oven to 200°C/180°C fan/400°F/gas mark 6.

Drain the nuts thoroughly and transfer to a blender or food processor together with the soya milk, miso paste, nutritional yeast, garlic, mustard and lemon juice. Blitz until completely smooth. Transfer to a saucepan and set over a medium heat. Bring to simmering point and cook for 6-8 minutes, stirring constantly, until thick and creamy. Remove from the heat, combine with the cooked pasta and season to taste. Transfer to a medium casserole dish. Scatter over the breadcrumbs, parsley leaves and paprika. Season again and drizzle over the olive oil.

Bake for 15-20 minutes until the breadcrumbs are crisp and golden. Serve immediately.

VEGETABLE KOFTA WRAPS

SERVES 4–6

You may instantly associate the word 'kofta' with lamb but get ready to see these little balls of happiness in a whole new light, vegan style. Full of vibrant veg and protein from the chickpeas, you've got well-rounded meals in these flavoursome koftas. I dip them in hummus and use them like a spoon, but you can top a flatbread with them and then go crazy adding coconut milk yoghurt, mixed leaves and a hummus of your choice.

For the koftas
200g sweet potato, peeled and grated

100g cauliflower florets

100g peas, frozen

1 carrot, grated

1 x 400g tin chickpeas, rinsed and drained

4 garlic cloves

1 tsp garam masala

1½ tsp ground cumin

1½ tsp ground coriander

3 tbsp gram flour

½-1 tsp dried chilli flakes, to taste

2 tsp sea salt

Sunflower oil, for frying

For the spicy yoghurt
4 tbsp soya milk yoghurt or coconut milk yoghurt

120g hummus

2 tsp harissa

To serve
Homemade flatbreads (page 79) or shop-bought flatbreads

Mixed salad leaves

Put all the kofta ingredients, apart from the sunflower oil, into a food processor and pulse on and off until the chickpeas and vegetables are very finely ground and the mixture holds together when pressed between your fingers. Take 2 tablespoons of the mixture and compact into a ball, then flatten slightly into a thick round. Place on a plate and continue with the rest of the mixture.

Place the yoghurt, hummus and harissa in a small bowl, stir to combine and set aside.

Preheat the oven to 110°C/90°C fan/225°F/gas mark ¼. Line a baking tray with kitchen paper.

To cook the koftas, cover the base of a medium non-stick frying pan with 1cm of oil and set over a medium-high heat. In batches, add in the koftas and fry for 3-4 minutes on each side, until deeply golden and cooked through. Transfer to the lined tray and keep warm in the oven while you cook the rest.

Heat the flatbreads in a toaster. Place the koftas on the bread, top with spicy yoghurt and serve with some mixed leaves.

PASTA WITH LENTIL BOLOGNESE

SERVES 4

I spend a lot of my time making up meaty Bolognese for my kids as it's one of the few meals all four kids will eat, so I thought it would be a fun challenge to switch it up into a vegan variety. The lentils work as a brilliant base in this dish as they feel meaty and substantial and give this dish a lot of protein and also flavour. I adore sundried tomatoes and they really do give this meal an extra something special.

2 tbsp extra virgin olive oil plus extra for drizzling

1 leek, trimmed and finely chopped

3 garlic cloves, thinly sliced

½ tsp ground cumin

400g tin lentils (any type), drained

400g passata

8 sundried tomatoes in oil, drained and finely chopped

50g pitted black olives, halved

300g wholegrain or wheat-free spaghetti

Small handful of flat leaf parsley, leaves only, roughly chopped

Sea salt and freshly ground black pepper

Put the oil into a pan and set over a medium heat. Add the leek and sauté for 8 minutes until softened. Add the garlic and cumin and fry for another 2 minutes. Add the lentils, passata, sundried tomatoes and olives and simmer for 15 minutes until thickened. Season well.

Meanwhile, bring a large pan of salted water to the boil and cook the spaghetti, according to the packet instructions. Drain well.

Divide the pasta between bowls and top with the sauce. Sprinkle with parsley and drizzle with extra virgin olive oil, to serve.

ITALIAN BRAISED CHICKPEAS WITH CAVOLO NERO AND ROSEMARY

SERVES 4

This dish is rich in flavour and nutritionally a winner as you have a lot of protein from the chickpeas and iron from the cavolo nero. If you can procure chickpeas in a glass jar from a local deli or health food shop, then they'll work better than the tinned variety in this particular recipe as they're much softer and more tender. If you can't find any locally just go for tinned chickpeas as they'll still make for a hearty and delicious lunch. Save any leftovers for dinner the next day or for lunch at work on a cold Monday.

3 tbsp extra virgin olive oil plus extra for drizzling

1 onion, finely chopped

1 tsp dried chilli flakes

6 garlic cloves, crushed

3 sprigs of fresh rosemary, leaves only, finely chopped

800g chickpeas, from a jar, or tinned, rinsed and drained

400g tin peeled plum tomatoes

500ml vegetable stock

150g cavolo nero, stalks removed and roughly chopped

Sea salt and freshly ground black pepper

Put the oil into a large pan and set over a medium heat. Add the onion, most of the chilli flakes and the garlic and rosemary and sauté gently for 10-12 minutes until the onions are soft and translucent. Stir frequently and reduce the heat if it looks like the garlic is beginning to catch.

Add the chickpeas, tomatoes and stock to the pan. Bring to a boil, then reduce the heat and simmer for 20 minutes. Season generously.

Add the cavolo nero and simmer for another 15 minutes. Taste and adjust the seasoning if necessary.

Serve in bowls with the remaining chilli flakes scattered over and a drizzle of olive oil.

SPINACH AND TOMATO GNOCCHI

SERVES 4

Making my own gnocchi has been a new venture and I've found it's really fun to make. This recipe is bursting with iron due to the spinach and the sauce is so warming and flavoursome it goes really well with the fluffy homemade gnocchi.

500g even-sized floury potatoes e.g. Desiree or Maris Piper

300g baby spinach

100g white spelt flour or Italian '00' flour plus extra for dusting

4 tbsp extra virgin olive oil plus extra for drizzling

400g cherry tomatoes, halved

4 garlic cloves, crushed

4 tbsp coconut cream

Handful of basil, leaves only

Sea salt and freshly ground black pepper

Bring a large pan of salted water to the boil and add the whole, unpeeled potatoes. Reduce the heat and simmer for 25 minutes until a sharp knife glides easily into the centre.

Meanwhile, place the spinach in a large pan over a high heat and cook, stirring frequently, until completely wilted down. Drain in a sieve and with the back of a spoon firmly press out as much water as possible. Transfer the spinach to a bowl and season well. Remove half the spinach, chop it very finely and set aside.

Once the potatoes are tender, remove to a colander, reserving the cooking water in the pan. Rub the skins off the hot potatoes, using a tea towel if they are too hot to handle. While the potatoes are still hot (otherwise the gnocchi will be tough), mash to a smooth consistency and season well.

Add the finely chopped spinach and flour to the mash and mix together until thoroughly combined. With clean dry hands knead the mixture and bring it together into a ball. Divide into quarters and roll out each piece, on a lightly floured board, into a long sausage shape. Cut the dough into 3cm long pieces. Bring the reserved potato cooking water back to the boil. Add the gnocchi, in batches, to the boiling water and cook for 2-3 minutes until they float to the surface. Remove from the pan with a slotted spoon and set aside. Repeat to cook the remaining gnocchi.

Put the oil into a large pan and set over a high heat. Once hot, add the tomatoes and fry for 5 minutes until blistered. Add the garlic, remaining cooked spinach and coconut cream and cook for 1 minute. Add the gnocchi and basil and gently stir to combine. Season to taste and serve immediately.

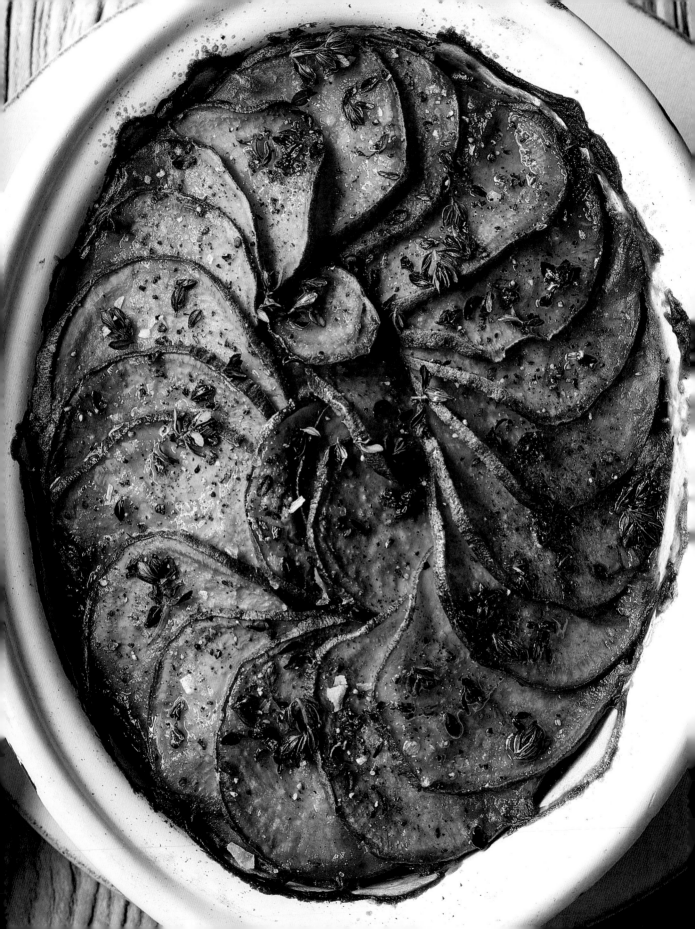

SQUASH, LENTIL, MUSHROOM AND THYME CASSEROLE

SERVES 4–6

This is one of my favourite Sunday lunch options. My mum is a vegetarian too and my husband has drastically cut out meat lately so it can feed the masses adequately, as well as adding that much needed comfort to a Sunday. It's full of veg and lentils so is easy on the gut and a dream for the taste buds. The perfect winter warmer that doesn't leave you in a lull.

2 onions, finely chopped

3 tbsp olive oil plus extra for drizzling

3 garlic cloves, crushed

2 tsp fresh thyme leaves

½ butternut squash, peeled, deseeded and cut into 2cm cubes

4 carrots, cut into 1cm cubes

200g shiitake mushrooms, thinly sliced

1 tbsp white spelt flour

500ml vegetable stock

100g red split lentils, washed

2 tbsp soy sauce

2 large sweet potatoes, thinly sliced

Sea salt and freshly ground black pepper

Salad or greens, to serve

Put the onions, oil, garlic and half the thyme leaves into a large pan and set over a medium-high heat. Sauté for 8 minutes, stirring frequently, until the onions are softened, taking care not to let them brown.

Stir in the squash, carrots, mushrooms and flour and fry for another 3-4 minutes, stirring constantly. Add the stock, lentils and soy sauce and bring to a boil. Reduce the heat and simmer for 25-30 minutes, stirring now and again, until the lentils are soft and the vegetables are almost tender. Season to taste.

Preheat the oven to 200°C/180°C fan/400°F/gas mark 6.

Bring a large pan of salted water to the boil and cook the sweet potato slices for 3 minutes. Drain thoroughly and lay out on a board.

Transfer the vegetable mixture into a large casserole dish and lay the sweet potato slices on top. Drizzle over some olive oil and scatter over the remaining thyme leaves. Season well and bake for 30-40 minutes, until golden on top and all the vegetables are tender.

Serve with a salad or some greens.

CREAMY NEW POTATO, CAULIFLOWER AND TURMERIC BAKE

SERVES 4–6

This comforting bake is a real Sunday soother. Something you can pop in the oven whilst you read the papers, its mouth-watering scent permeating your kitchen. Make sure to use soya milk rather than any other alternative milks as it has the correct consistency to ensure the creamy layer of the bake is velvety and thick. Turmeric brings such colour and warmth to a dish and the nutritional yeast provides the ultimate cheese flavour for any vegan.

800g new potatoes, halved

1.2kg cauliflower (roughly 2 small heads), cut into florets

10 garlic cloves

3 tbsp fresh thyme leaves

1 tsp ground turmeric

6 tbsp olive oil

3 tbsp nutritional yeast

1 tbsp miso paste

300ml unsweetened soya milk

Sea salt and freshly ground black pepper

Green salad, to serve

Preheat the oven to 200°C/180°C fan/400°F/gas mark 6.

Put the new potatoes, cauliflower, whole garlic cloves, 2 tablespoons of the thyme, the turmeric and olive oil into a large roasting tray and season with 1½ teaspoons of salt and plenty of pepper. Toss everything together until evenly coated and roast for 25 minutes, mixing half way through, until just tender.

Place a third of the potato and cauliflower mixture into a food processor with the nutritional yeast and miso paste and blitz to a rough purée. Slowly pour in the milk with the motor running until you have a smooth purée. Season to taste.

Build layers of whole potatoes and cauliflower and spoonfuls of the vegetable purée into a medium-sized casserole dish, finishing with some of the whole vegetables and the remaining thyme. Bake for 10-15 minutes until golden and tender.

Serve with a green salad.

MOROCCAN CHICKPEA AND LENTIL STEW

SERVES 6–8

The smell of this stew is enough to make your nose hairs tingle, your taste buds dance and your stomach twitch with anticipation. I love stews as they're easy to make and can sit flavour absorbing and slowly cooking whilst you get on with other kitchen-based chores.

3 tbsp extra virgin olive oil plus extra to serve

1 onion, finely chopped

2 celery stalks, finely chopped

2 carrots, finely chopped

2 red chillies, deseeded and finely chopped

4 garlic cloves, crushed

1 tbsp cumin seeds

2 tsp ground turmeric

2 tsp sweet smoked paprika

2 tsp ground cinnamon

2cm piece of fresh ginger, peeled and finely grated

3 tbsp tomato purée

1 litre vegetable stock

2 x 400g tins chopped tomatoes

2 x 400g tins chickpeas, rinsed and drained

150g brown or green lentils

Large handful of flat leaf parsley, leaves only

Sea salt and freshly ground black pepper

To serve
Lemon wedges
Sourdough bread

Put the olive oil into a large pan set over a medium heat. Add the onion, celery, carrots and chillies and sauté for 8 minutes, until the onions have softened. Add the garlic, all the dried spices, ginger and tomato purée and cook for another 2 minutes, stirring all the time, until aromatic.

Add the stock, tomatoes, chickpeas and lentils and bring to a boil, then reduce the heat a little and simmer gently, stirring frequently, for 40-45 minutes, until the lentils are tender and the stew has thickened a little.

Stir in most of the parsley and season to taste with up to 2 teaspoons of salt (depending on how salty the stock is) and black pepper. Ladle into bowls, drizzle over a little extra virgin olive oil and sprinkle over the remaining parsley. Serve with the lemon wedges, to squeeze over, and some bread, to dunk.

BUTTERNUT SQUASH, EDAMAME AND SPINACH GRAIN BOWL

SERVES 4

Butternut squash takes a little while to cook so this is a good weekend lunch, leaving you with a warming and luxurious meal that will give you energy and a spring in your step.

You can use any grains you like or have in your cupboards at home from quinoa to spelt or durum wheat or try using a pack of mixed grains which a lot of supermarkets now sell. Butternut squash is an excellent source of vitamin C, and the added spinach is a great way to get some iron in your system, too.

1 butternut squash, peeled, halved and deseeded

5 tbsp olive oil

200g edamame beans

500g ready-to-eat mixed grains (any type)

150g cherry tomatoes, halved

60g baby spinach

Sea salt and freshly ground black pepper

For the dressing

2 garlic cloves, peeled and crushed

2cm piece of fresh ginger, peeled and grated

3 tbsp cashew butter

2 tbsp soy sauce

2 tbsp apple cider vinegar

2 tbsp extra virgin olive oil

Preheat the oven to 200°C/180°C fan/400°F/gas mark 6.

Cut the squash into small bite-size pieces. Place on a large baking tray and toss in 2 tablespoons of the olive oil. Season well and roast in the oven for 35 minutes or until tender and golden.

Meanwhile, cook the edamame beans in a pan of boiling salted water for 5 minutes until tender. Drain and set aside.

For the dressing, put all the ingredients into a bowl and whisk until smooth.

When ready to serve, heat the mixed grains, according to the packet instructions, and divide between bowls. Top with the squash, edamame, tomatoes, spinach and dollops of the dressing.

Most nights by the time I have wrangled my kids into bed and begged them to stay put, I am wrecked. My brain capacity has diminished and my energy is at an all-time low. It can be easy to fall in to bad habits if you have a similar schedule to me, juggling work or children or indeed both. Our days can be long, so the temptation to order a takeaway or eat a ready-made meal is overwhelming. Nothing wrong with doing that now and again, but choosing to eat mostly vegan means I have to make a lot of my meals from scratch, which can only ever be a good thing.

This chapter is dedicated to those of you who struggle in the evenings to make good choices, myself included, yet want to still feel you're putting something decent in your system. The recipes are designed to be simple and easy yet packed with flavour and nutrients to keep you going until bed time. I've also tried to consider those of you who are very new to vegan food by giving you interesting alternatives to those meals you might usually dash towards at the end of a long day. My husband's go to meal after a tiring day, whether in takeaway form or home cooked is a curry, so you'll find a Broccoli katsu curry (page 124) that should round off your day nicely without too much cooking fuss.

You can also impress your partner or flatmate with the Black bean sausages (page 126) and Mixed root mash (page 128) which I so enjoyed creating. I have wanted to nail a homemade sausage for some time and am really pretty chuffed with how these turned out. They're bursting with flavour and fibre as well as potassium from the black beans. We all need nice amounts of fibre in our lives so get these saucy sausages in your life asap!

A lot of these meals can also be cooked up and then saved for the next day if you live by yourself or have made too much. You can heat them up and have them for lunch the following day or if you make the Flatbread pizzas (page 120), they're good cold, too.

I hope this chapter really proves to you that eating vegan needn't be boring, a faff or a huge compromise.

Dishy
DINNERS

COCONUT CREAM SPINACH PASTA

SERVES 4

This is beyond easy and quick to make but doesn't skip on flavour. Use whichever pasta you prefer, I always like to use brown rice pasta as I love the taste and it's a good carbohydrate for my kids to eat too. The spinach also ensures you'll get some good greens in your kids if you make this as a family meal. You can buy coconut cream in most supermarkets now but if you can't find it buy a normal tin of coconut milk and use the creamy, more solidified layer at the top of the can.

360g macaroni, ditaloni or boccole or other short tube pasta

250g baby spinach

30g basil leaves

1 tbsp miso paste

2 garlic cloves, crushed

200ml coconut cream

2 tbsp tahini

1 tbsp balsamic vinegar

2 tsp dried chilli flakes (optional)

Sea salt and freshly ground black pepper

Bring a large pan of salted water to the boil and cook the pasta, according to the packet instructions.

Meanwhile, put the remaining ingredients, apart from the dried chilli, into a food processor and blitz until smooth. Season to taste.

Drain the pasta, reserving a cup of the cooking water. Return the pasta to the hot dry pan and stir in the spinach mixture and enough of the reserved pasta water to create a thick, creamy sauce. Taste and adjust the seasoning, if necessary.

Serve with the dried chilli flakes scattered over, if using.

FLATBREAD PIZZAS WITH BASIL AND CHICKPEA PESTO, ROCKET AND CHERRY TOMATOES

SERVES 2

If you've enjoyed making the flatbreads (page 79) this is another way to enjoy them. We love to make pizzas in our house as the kids have great fun picking their own toppings and enjoy being part of the cooking process. The homemade pesto gives so much flavour and you can be as wild or refined as you desire when topping these bad boys up. If you've also had a bash at the vegan cheese (page 99) you can add dollops of this to your flatbread base for a more traditional pizza recipe.

1 garlic clove, crushed

Large handful of basil, leaves only plus extra to serve

20g cashews, roasted for 5 minutes at 180°C fan until golden

50g tinned chickpeas

2 tbsp passata

5 tbsp extra virgin olive oil plus extra to serve

2 homemade flatbreads (page 79) or shop-bought flatbreads

20 cherry tomatoes, halved

100g Vegan cheesy dip (page 56) or shop-bought vegan cheese-style block

30g rocket

Sea salt and freshly ground black pepper

Preheat the oven to 220°C/200°C fan/450°F/gas mark 8.

Put the garlic, basil, cashews, chickpeas, passata and olive oil into a food processor and blitz to form a rough paste. Season to taste.

Place the flatbreads on a baking tray. Divide the pesto between the bases and spread it out evenly. Arrange the tomatoes and spoon the cheesy dip or crumble the cheese-style block over the pesto and bake for 7-9 minutes until the base is crispy and the tomatoes have softened.

Serve with the rocket and extra basil leaves scattered over and a drizzle of olive oil.

TOMATO, FENNEL AND BEAN BAKE

SERVES 4

~~~~~~

I feel sorry for fennel. It always seems to get a little left out but it's so packed with flavour and, when remembered, makes a gorgeous addition to vegan dishes. In this bake, its unique flavour doesn't overpower the dish but instead complements the tomatoes and beans beautifully. It's a wholesome and comforting meal that will please the masses and become a firm family favourite.

3 tbsp extra virgin olive oil plus extra for drizzling

1 onion, finely chopped

1 carrot, finely chopped

1 fennel bulb, outer leaves removed, trimmed and finely chopped

4 garlic cloves, crushed

2 tsp ground cumin

1 tsp ground coriander

1 tsp sweet smoked paprika

400g black eyed beans, drained

2 x 400g tins chopped tomatoes

2 tbsp soy sauce

1 tbsp red wine vinegar

6 tbsp fresh breadcrumbs

3 tbsp nutritional yeast

Sea salt and freshly ground black pepper

Salad or steamed green vegetables, to serve

Put the oil into a wide flameproof casserole dish and set over a medium-high heat. Add the onion, carrot and fennel and sauté for 8 minutes, stirring frequently, until softened but not browned. Add the garlic, cumin, coriander and half the paprika and cook for another 2-3 minutes until aromatic.

Preheat the oven to 200°C/180°C fan/400°F/gas mark 6.

Add the beans, tomatoes and soy sauce and bring to a boil. Reduce the heat and simmer for 20 minutes, stirring frequently, until thickened. Add the vinegar and season to taste.

Combine together the breadcrumbs, nutritional yeast and remaining paprika and scatter over the top of the casserole. Bake for 10-15 minutes until golden. Remove, drizzle over a little more olive oil and serve immediately.

Serve with a salad or some steamed green vegetables, if you'd prefer.

BROCCOLI KATSU CURRY

SERVES 4

This is weirdly simple. It sounds and looks like it might be time consuming or complicated but once you've tried this recipe you'll see just how easy it is. I adore roasted broccoli and it works so well in this curry. The more veg the better and you're certainly getting your fill with this dish. The sauce will make your taste buds dance and you'll feel full, yet not sluggish in the slightest, after devouring this incredible dinner.

3 tbsp olive oil

1 onion, finely chopped

2 carrots, cut into 1cm pieces

3 garlic cloves, crushed

3cm piece of fresh ginger, peeled and grated

1 tbsp mild curry powder

1 tsp garam masala

½ tsp ground turmeric

1 tbsp white spelt flour

400ml vegetable stock

1 tbsp soy sauce

350g Tenderstem® broccoli

100g fresh breadcrumbs

3 spring onions, finely chopped

Sea salt and freshly ground black pepper, to taste

Brown rice, to serve

Put half the oil into a pan and place over a medium heat. Add the onion, carrots, garlic and ginger and cook gently for 8 minutes, stirring frequently, until the onions are translucent, taking care not to let anything burn.

Add the curry powder, garam masala, turmeric and flour and stir-fry for another 2 minutes until fragrant. Gradually stir in the stock and soy sauce and bring to a boil. Reduce the heat and simmer for 10 minutes, stirring frequently, until thickened and the carrots are cooked through.

Using a handheld or upright blender, blitz the sauce until completely smooth, adding in a little water if it is too thick. Season to taste.

Preheat the oven to 200°C/180°C fan/400°F/gas mark 6. Line a baking tray with foil or baking parchment.

Toss the broccoli in the remaining oil, to coat, and season well. Roll in the breadcrumbs until evenly coated, transfer to the lined baking tray and roast for 10-15 minutes until golden and the broccoli is cooked through.

Divide the sauce between your plates and top with the katsu broccoli. Scatter the spring onions on top and serve with rice.

BLACK BEAN SAUSAGES

MAKES 10–12 SAUSAGES

It was my mission when brainstorming this book to come up with a decent vegan sausage recipe and I'm pretty chuffed with this one. Black beans make the perfect base for these vegan delights and also make them look a little like traditional sausages, too. The smoked tofu and sundried tomatoes give them a real meaty flavour and they're wonderful served with the Mixed root mash (page 128).

2 tbsp olive oil, plus extra for frying

1 onion, finely chopped

3 garlic cloves, crushed

1 tsp thyme leaves

1 tsp finely chopped fresh rosemary leaves

1 x 400g tin black beans, rinsed and drained

6 sundried tomatoes in oil, drained

1 carrot, finely grated

200g smoked tofu, drained and grated

3 tbsp rice flour, sifted

Sea salt and freshly ground black pepper

Mixed root mash (page 128), to serve

Preheat the oven to 200°C/180°C fan/gas mark 6 and line a baking tray with parchment paper.

Put 2 tablespoons of oil into a pan and set over a medium heat. Sauté the onion for 8 minutes until soft and translucent, but not coloured. Add the garlic, thyme leaves and rosemary leaves and fry for another 2 minutes, until aromatic. Season to taste.

Put the black beans and sundried tomatoes into a food processor and blitz to form a rough paste. Remove to a bowl and stir in the onion mixture, carrot, tofu and flour. Season to taste.

Take 3 tablespoons of the mixture (around 75g) and mould it into a sausage shape, compacting it firmly with your hands. Repeat with the rest of the mixture to make 10-12 sausages.

Heat the remaining oil in a non-stick frying pan, over a medium heat, and fry the sausages for about 6 minutes, turning now and then, until golden. Transfer to the lined baking tray and roast for 10 minutes until cooked through.

Serve the sausages with Mixed root mash.

MIXED ROOT MASH

SERVES 4, AS A SIDE

My mum cannot stand mashed potatoes. I think it reminds her of school (quite a long time ago but hey these things can really stick with us!). So, in honour of Lin Cotton's dislike of the school dinner fave, I have whizzed up this recipe of vibrant root vegetables to put a spin on this classic. Delicious served with the Black bean sausages (page 126).

3 carrots, roughly chopped

2 large sweet potato, roughly chopped

½ swede, roughly chopped

2 tbsp coconut oil

1 tbsp extra virgin olive oil

Sea salt and freshly ground black pepper

Bring a large pan of salted water to the boil. Add the carrots, sweet potato and swede and simmer for 20-25 minutes, until tender. Drain thoroughly and return to the pan with the coconut and olive oil. Mash to a rough mash consistency and season to taste with salt and pepper. Serve immediately.

FRIED COURGETTE WITH ROASTED PEPPERS, PEANUTS AND CHILLI

SERVES 8–10

This dish has a real Eastern flavour to it and it's surprisingly quick to whip up. Courgettes can often be discarded in favour of heartier veg as they can be quite watery but they work really well in this recipe and provide lots of fibre plus vitamins B6 and C. Serve it up in bowls with rice, quinoa or straight up.

3 large courgettes, halved lengthways

4 tbsp olive oil

300g roasted red peppers, from a jar, drained and thinly sliced

4 garlic cloves, crushed

2 tsp cumin seeds

2 tbsp soy sauce

2 tsp rice vinegar

1 tsp dried chilli flakes

Small handful of Thai basil, leaves only, roughly chopped

Small handful of roasted peanuts (salted or unsalted), roughly chopped

Sea salt and freshly ground black pepper

Brown rice or quinoa, to serve

Cut the courgette into 1cm slices on an angle. Put the olive oil in a large pan and set over a high heat. When very hot, add the courgette and stir-fry for 2 minutes. Add the red peppers and fry for another 2-3 minutes, until the courgette is golden.

Turn down the heat, add the garlic and cumin seeds and fry for another 1-2 minutes until aromatic. Add the soy sauce, rice vinegar, chilli, basil and peanuts and toss to combine. Season to taste.

Serve immediately with brown rice or quinoa.

TOFU TIKKA MASALA

SERVES 4

My husband, Jesse, loves a tikka masala, so this one is for him. Super creamy due to the coconut milk yoghurt and coconut cream and full of flavour and spice, this meal will leave you feeling satisfied, energised and suitably smug that you made it from scratch. Serve with rice or naan bread on a chilly evening.

4 tbsp sunflower oil

800g firm tofu, drained and cut into bite-size pieces

3 tsp garam masala

1 tsp ground turmeric

2 onions, finely chopped

4cm piece of fresh ginger, peeled and grated

6 garlic cloves, crushed

1 tsp ground cumin

1 tsp sweet smoked paprika

2 tbsp tomato purée

400g tin chopped tomatoes

150ml coconut milk yoghurt

150ml coconut cream

1 tbsp lemon juice

Small handful of coriander, leaves only

Sea salt and freshly ground black pepper

Rice and/or vegan naan bread, to serve

Put half the oil into a large pan and set over a medium-high heat. Add the tofu, half the garam masala and half the turmeric, 1 teaspoon of salt and half a teaspoon of black pepper. Toss everything together, and fry for 5 minutes until golden and fragrant. Remove to a bowl and return the pan to the heat.

Add the remaining oil and the onions to the pan and fry for 6-8 minutes until translucent and soft. Add the ginger and garlic, lower the heat and fry for a further 5 minutes until aromatic. Add the remaining garam masala and remaining turmeric, cumin, smoked paprika, tomato purée and chopped tomatoes to the pan, bring to a boil, then reduce the heat and simmer for 5 minutes. Stir in the yoghurt, coconut cream and lemon juice. Taste and adjust the seasoning with more salt and pepper. If you like you can purée the sauce at this point, or simply leave it as it is. Stir the tofu back into the sauce and warm through.

Serve immediately with the coriander sprinkled over and rice and/or naan bread on the side.

GINGER AND MISO TOFU WITH NOODLES

SERVES 4

This is mega quick to cook and a really lovely way to end your day if you've arrived home from work after a long day and a stressful journey or are bedraggled from putting the kids to bed. We love soba noodles in our house as they cook quickly and the kids love them too. This nutty dressing is one of my favourite flavours and you can make it as spicy or mild as you desire.

For the sauce

2 tbsp toasted sesame oil

3 garlic cloves, crushed

2cm piece of fresh ginger, peeled and finely grated

2 tbsp soy sauce

1½ tbsp miso paste

1½ tbsp maple syrup

2 tbsp crunchy peanut butter

3 tbsp rice vinegar

1 tbsp sriracha chilli sauce

1 tbsp sesame seeds, roasted

4 spring onions, finely chopped

For the noodles, broccoli and tofu

200g broccoli, broken into florets

300g soba noodles

400g firm tofu, drained and cut into 2cm cubes

To make the sauce, in a large bowl combine the sesame oil, garlic, ginger, soy sauce, miso paste, maple syrup, peanut butter, vinegar and chilli sauce. Add most of the sesame seeds and most of the spring onions to the bowl, reserving the remainder to scatter over later. Whisk together until smooth.

Bring a large pan of salted water to the boil and cook the broccoli, for 3-4 minutes, until tender. Remove with a slotted spoon, keeping the water on the boil.

Add the noodles to the boiling water and cook, according to the packet instructions, until just tender, taking care not to overcook them. Drain the noodles and immediately transfer to a large bowl of cold water and thoroughly wash the noodles with your hands under more running cold water to remove the starchy coating from cooking. Drain thoroughly, place in a bowl and pour over half the sauce, stirring to combine.

Add the tofu cubes to the bowl with the remaining sauce and stir to coat. Place a large pan over a medium-high heat and add the tofu and sauce. Stir-fry for 3 minutes, then add the cold noodles and sauce and fry for another 2-3 minutes, tossing now and again, until hot.

Divide the noodles between bowls and serve with the broccoli and the remaining sesame seeds and spring onions scattered over.

CURRIED LENTIL, TENDERSTEM BROCCOLI, SPRING ONION AND RED PEPPER SALAD

SERVES 4

When I'm short on time or exhausted after putting the kids to bed, the last thing I want to do is make dinner for myself and my husband. To ward us off eating a bowl of late night cereal, I usually make up a hearty and vibrant salad to send hunger running and to stop midnight snacking. It's a pretty quick salad to make but is still comforting due to the chargrilled spring onion and broccoli.

250g Tenderstem® broccoli

8 spring onions, trimmed

4 tbsp extra virgin olive oil

2 tsp mild curry powder

2 garlic cloves, crushed

2 tsp balsamic vinegar

1 tsp maple syrup

250g pack cooked Puy lentils

4 roasted red peppers from a jar, drained and thinly sliced

120g mixed leaves

Small handful of basil, leaves only

1 tsp dried chilli flakes

Sea salt and freshly ground black pepper

Bring a large pan of salted water to the boil and cook the broccoli for 4-6 minutes, until just tender, but not limp. Drain and set aside.

Place a griddle pan over a medium-high heat. Toss the spring onions in 1 tablespoon of olive oil and season well. Add to the pan and cook for 6-8 minutes, turning now and again until tender and charred.

Put the curry powder into a dry pan and set over a medium heat. Cook for 2–3 minutes, shaking the pan now and again, until the curry powder is roasted and aromatic. Transfer the powder to a bowl. Add 1 tablespoon of olive oil and the garlic to the pan and fry for 1 minute until aromatic. Add the garlic to the bowl with the curry powder and stir in the remaining olive oil, the vinegar and maple syrup. Season to taste.

Heat the lentils, according to the packet instructions. Combine with half the dressing and arrange on a large serving dish with the red pepper, mixed leaves and basil tangled in amongst them. Layer the broccoli and spring onions on top, scatter over the dried chilli flakes and drizzle over the remaining dressing. Serve immediately.

GARLIC AND PAK CHOI FRIED RICE

SERVES 4

Fried rice is such a brilliant quick and easy meal if, like in our house, you have rice left over from the day before. I often cook too much for the kids and then store the leftovers in the fridge. It's important you cool leftover cooked rice to room temperature within an hour of cooking – remove it from the pan and place in a shallow airtight container. Once cool pop a lid on and chill in the fridge. You need rice that has been in the fridge overnight for fried rice as it needs to be hard and cold to really crisp up well, but do make sure you only reheat it once and that it is piping hot before you tuck in.

5 tbsp sunflower oil

8 garlic cloves, very thinly sliced

1 tsp toasted sesame oil

1 tbsp rice vinegar

4cm piece of fresh ginger, peeled and very finely chopped

300g pak choi, cut into strips

800g cooked white rice or ready-cooked pouch

4 spring onions, finely sliced

Sea salt and freshly ground black pepper

1 red chilli, deseeded and thinly sliced

Put the sunflower oil into a large non-stick pan and set over a medium heat. When it is hot, add the sliced garlic and stir-fry for 3-5 minutes, depending on the heat of the oil, until golden and crispy. Remove with a slotted spoon and leave to drain on kitchen paper.

Add the sesame oil and rice vinegar to the pan and increase the heat to high. Add the ginger and stir-fry for 1 minute, then add the pak choi and rice. Spread out the rice and firmly press it down against the base of the pan. Leave it to crisp up for a few minutes, then toss together and repeat this process a few more times until the rice is crisp and golden in places and the pak choi is vibrant green.

Stir in most of the spring onions and season the rice, to taste. Transfer the rice to a large plate and serve with the fried garlic, chilli and remaining spring onions scattered over.

TOFU FINGERS WITH SWEET POTATO WEDGES

SERVES 4

I loved fish fingers and chips as a kid and my kids still adore them now so I thought it would be fun to have a bash at making a vegan version. Tofu is so versatile and works brilliantly in a vegan diet as it's a good source of protein, so I've based the faux fish fingers on this vegan staple. The sweet potato wedges are simple to make and chunky in appearance and flavour. It's an all-round winner.

4 sweet potatoes, cut into wedges

4 tbsp olive oil

700g smoked tofu, drained

250g medium oatmeal

Sea salt and freshly ground black pepper

To serve
Tomato ketchup
Green salad

Preheat the oven to 200°C/180°C fan/400°F/gas mark 6. Line two baking trays with baking parchment.

Toss the sweet potato wedges in half the oil, season well and transfer to one of the lined baking trays. Roast for 25-30 minutes until tender and golden.

Cut the tofu into 2 x 7cm pieces. Toss in the remaining oil and season generously. Roll the oiled tofu fingers in the oatmeal and transfer to the remaining baking tray. Add to the oven with the potatoes and cook for 20 minutes, until golden and crispy. The sweet potato wedges and tofu fingers should be finished cooking at approximately the same time.

Remove from the oven and sprinkle over a little more seasoning, then serve immediately with ketchup and a green salad.

CAULIFLOWER STEAKS WITH PINE NUT AND PARSLEY OIL

SERVES 2

Cauliflowers are so versatile and perfect for a vegan diet. Long gone are the days of cauliflower being over boiled by your nan and then served to a disgruntled face. Cauliflower steaks are one of my favourite ways to jazz up this previously out-of-favour veg and the pine nut and parsley oil really gives a lot of punch to this simple yet yummy dinner. You can also use the leftover cauliflower in the Cauliflower rice salad with cannellini beans, avocado and radishes (page 74) or in the Rice and veggie bowl (page 84).

40g pine nuts

3 tbsp extra virgin olive oil

1 tsp maple syrup

Pinch of dried chilli flakes

1 tbsp red wine vinegar

Small handful of flat leaf parsley, leaves only, roughly chopped

1 cauliflower

Sea salt and freshly ground black pepper

Salad, to serve

Preheat the oven to 200°C/180°C fan/400°F/gas mark 6.

Spread the pine nuts out on a baking tray and roast for 3-5 minutes, until golden. Cool and roughly chop. Stir in 2 tablespoons of the olive oil, the maple syrup, dried chilli flakes, vinegar and parsley. Season to taste and set aside.

Trim the base off the cauliflower and sit it on a chopping board. Cut two 2cm thick steaks from the middle of the cauliflower, slicing vertically through the centre of the vegetable, so the central core holds the steak together. Keep the remaining cauliflower for another time.

Place the steaks on a baking tray and coat with the remaining olive oil. Season well and roast for 20-25 minutes, carefully turning once, half way through cooking, until golden and tender.

Serve the steaks with the pine nut and parsley oil spooned over and some salad on the side.

Creating your own banquet-style setting really does cut out a lot of awkwardness if you have guests over. No worrying about portion size or preference, just unadulterated feasting heaven. This kind of dining experience will forever be my favourite way to cook for other people. It takes me back to my childhood where no family gathering would be complete without at least one kitchen counter being turned in to a quiche bearing buffet. My mum and aunties are still very keen on multiple dishes to choose from to mitigate any awkwardness or faff of having to serve up individual plates. I have inherited this trait and buffet it up at any given opportunity.

Mismatched crockery embracing mountains of gleaming potatoes, decade-old plates smothered in rainbow coloured veg and knives ready to messily cut into freshly baked steaming pies. Dining room chairs are ditched and sofa arms are instead perched on and conversation flows freely as everyone clambers back for seconds and sometimes thirds. Often in these situations I won't even tell my guests that what they're eating is vegan. It matters not as what they're experiencing is a shared enjoyment of tasty and comforting food. The fact that I've used tofu instead of chicken or pulses instead of mince is luckily not the focus as these recipes all hold a little vegan feasting magic.

The Jackfruit burgers and slaw (page 145) are always a total hit especially for those still wondering how vegan food can be filling or hearty. These juicy, flavour-rammed burgers are so decadent and dreamy and are a great way to introduce a first time jackfruit eater to this very versatile vegan fave. My Aunty Karen makes a mean chilli so this sharing feast chapter would not be complete without my vegan version, Mixed bean chilli (page 151), to enjoy.

Get the gang round, the mismatch serving plates and bowls out, and get feasting.

SHARING FEASTS

JACKFRUIT BURGERS AND SLAW

SERVES 4

Jackfruit only came in to my life in the last 12 months. I was dubious on the first try to say the least. I didn't like how it looked and was confused that it could feel so meaty. Now I'm a die-hard fan and love its many guises -- the perfect substitute for pulled pork, meat in burgers and even tuna depending on how you flavour it. You can buy it in a tin or vacuum pack in many supermarkets. This is a simple recipe if it's your first try and works perfectly with the slaw. Great for a slouchy, hearty meal or make in smaller portions for mini burgers.

For the slaw

¼ red cabbage, cored and shredded

¼ red onion, finely sliced

1 carrot, grated

1 apple, cored and grated

1 tsp Dijon mustard

2 tsp sherry vinegar

1 tbsp extra virgin olive oil

Small handful of flat leaf parsley, leaves only, finely chopped

Sea salt and freshly ground black pepper

For the burgers

2 x 400g tins jackfruit

2 tbsp olive oil

3 garlic cloves, crushed

200ml BBQ sauce

4 burger buns, halved

Small handful of rocket

In a large bowl, combine together all of the slaw ingredients and season well. Set aside.

Drain and thoroughly rinse the jackfruit, then wrap in a clean tea towel and squeeze out as much liquid as possible. Put the oil into a non-stick pan and set over a high heat. Add the jackfruit and stir-fry for 4-5 minutes, until beginning to colour. Add the garlic and fry for another minute until aromatic. Add the BBQ sauce, reduce the heat and simmer gently, stirring frequently, for 25-30 minutes, until the sauce is thick and the jackfruit is tender. Once tender, use two forks to shred the jackfruit.

Preheat the grill to high. Toast the inside of the burger buns under the grill. Top the bases of the buns with the rocket and a little of the slaw. Add some pulled jackfruit and some more slaw on top. Finish with the tops of the buns and serve immediately.

NUT ROAST

SERVES 6

A decent nut roast is hard to come by but is now an essential at our family Christmas. It's the tradition that I am always in charge of. I say tradition – I've actually made it one as I so love making a nut roast and am very obsessive about the outcome. It's got to be juicy, flavoursome and hearty and this one ticks all the boxes. The majority of this nut roast is veg, which in my eyes is how it should be to ensure it's not too stodgy or dry. The nuts offer up flavour and protein and the herbs bring it all together. The perfect dish for a Sunday roast, Christmas day or Thanksgiving.

60g pecans

60g hazelnuts

60g cashews

300g sweet potato, roughly chopped

3 parsnips, about 400g, roughly chopped

3 tbsp olive oil

1 onion, finely chopped

2 celery stalks, very finely chopped

300g chestnut mushrooms, finely sliced

3 garlic cloves, crushed

1 tsp sweet smoked paprika

1 tsp ground cumin

100g fresh breadcrumbs

4 tbsp nutritional yeast

2 tbsp soy sauce

2 tbsp gram flour

Small bunch of sage, leaves only, finely chopped, about 2 tbsp

Preheat the oven to 200°C/180°C fan/400°F/gas mark 6. Line the loaf tin fully with baking parchment.

Put the nuts on a baking tray and roast for 5 minutes until a shade darker and aromatic. Remove from the tray and set aside.

Place the sweet potato and parsnips on the baking tray, drizzle over half the oil and toss to coat. Season generously and roast for 25-30 minutes until tender and golden.

While the vegetables are roasting, put the remaining olive oil into a frying pan and set over a medium-high heat. Add the onion and celery and cook for 5 minutes, then add in the mushrooms and garlic and fry for 10 minutes, stirring frequently, until the onions and celery have softened and the mushrooms have browned. If there is still any liquid in the pan, continue cooking until it has all evaporated and the ingredients are mostly dry. Take care not to let the mixture burn. Add the paprika and cumin and season generously, to taste.

Remove the sweet potato and parsnips from the oven, but leave the oven turned on. Transfer the sweet potato and parsnip to a bowl and mash half of it. Roughly chop the nuts and add most of them to bowl. Add the onion mixture, breadcrumbs, nutritional yeast, soy sauce, gram flour and chopped sage.

Thoroughly combine everything together, taste and adjust the seasoning if necessary.

Small handful of flat leaf
parsley, leaves only,
roughly chopped

Sea salt and freshly ground
black pepper

Extra virgin olive oil, to
serve

Special equipment needed
900g loaf tin

Transfer the mixture to the lined loaf tin and press down
firmly with the back of a spoon. Cover with foil and roast for
40 minutes, then remove the foil and roast for a further 20
minutes. Remove and leave to cool in the tin for 20 minutes,
then carefully turn out onto a serving board.

Combine the remaining chopped nuts with the parsley and
spoon down the centre of the nut roast. Drizzle with a little extra
virgin olive oil and serve immediately.

ORANGE ROASTED CARROTS

SERVES 6, AS A SIDE

I just adore the marriage of flavours in this exceptional side dish – I find them
particularly addictive, which isn't such a bad addiction to have, I guess. It is a great
accompaniment if you have a main course sorted or works well if you are serving
your mates loads of dishes – the perfect way to bring carrots to the party!

600g carrots, halved
lengthways

2 tbsp extra virgin olive oil

Zest and juice of 1 orange

1 tbsp maple syrup

Sea salt and freshly ground
black pepper

Preheat the oven to 200°C/180°C fan/400°F/gas mark 6.

Place the carrots on a large baking tray and toss with the oil,
orange zest and juice and maple syrup. Season well, cover
tightly with foil and roast for 15 minutes.

Remove the foil and continue roasting for 15-20 minutes until
tender and slightly caramelised. Serve immediately.

MIXED BEAN CHILLI WITH FLATBREADS

SERVES 4

My Aunty Karen is the queen of chilli and always makes big delicious meaty and vegetarian options when we head round to hers. This dish delivers as much sass and flavour as my auntie's version, as it's bursting with spices and flavour. Once again, those good old beans provide a ton of very important protein, too. Perfect served with homemade flatbreads (page 79) or shop-bought flatbreads or rice.

2 tbsp olive oil

1 onion, finely chopped

3 garlic cloves, crushed

1-2 tsp ancho or chipotle chilli paste

1 red pepper, deseeded and finely chopped

1 tsp ground cumin

1 tsp ground coriander

1 tsp sweet smoked paprika

2 tbsp tomato purée

400g tin chopped tomatoes

350ml vegetable stock

400g tin kidney beans, rinsed and drained

400g tin black beans, rinsed and drained

4 homemade flatbreads (page 79) or shop-bought flatbreads

Sea salt and freshly ground black pepper

To serve

Soya milk or coconut milk yoghurt

Coriander or flat leaf parsley leaves

Lime wedges

Put the oil into a large pan and set over a medium-high heat. Add the onion and sauté for 8 minutes until translucent. Add the garlic and cook for another minute until aromatic. Add 1-2 teaspoons of chilli paste, according to taste and the red pepper, cumin, coriander, smoked paprika and tomato purée and stir fry for another 3 minutes. Season well.

Add the chopped tomatoes, stock and beans and bring to a boil. Reduce the heat and simmer for 30 minutes, stirring now and again, until slightly thickened. Season, to taste.

Warm the flatbreads in a toaster or oven. Serve the chilli in bowls with a little yoghurt dolloped on top, the coriander or parsley scattered over and the flatbreads and lime wedges on the side.

CARAMELISED BUTTERNUT SQUASH WITH BALSAMIC ROASTED TOMATOES

SERVES 4

A gorgeous dish to make if you have mates over for dinner. It's low-fuss but high in taste and full of goodness. Butternut squash is full of vitamin C and fibre and is a very versatile veg to cook with. I love balsamic and would happily drink it from the bottle. Its tartness gives edge to the sweetness of the squash. If you're not 100 per cent vegan this is also very nice with feta sprinkled over the top of the squash once out of the oven.

2 butternut squash

5 tbsp olive oil

300g cherry tomatoes, halved

2 garlic cloves, crushed

2 tbsp balsamic vinegar plus extra for drizzling

Small handful of basil, leaves only, roughly chopped

Sea salt and freshly ground black pepper

Preheat the oven to 180°C/160°C fan/350°F/gas mark 4.

Cut each squash in half lengthways and scoop out the seeds, no need to peel. Place on a large baking tray and coat with 4 tablespoons of the olive oil. Season well and roast in the oven for 35 minutes.

Combine together the tomatoes, garlic, remaining olive oil, balsamic vinegar and season well. After 35 minutes add to the tray with the squash and continue cooking for another 15-20 minutes until the squash are golden and a sharp knife glides easily into the flesh and the tomatoes have burst open and released their juices.

Place the squash on a platter with the tomatoes on top and the basil leaves scattered over and another little drizzle of balsamic vinegar, to serve.

SESAME COATED TOFU

SERVES 4

Many folk out there still don't 'get' tofu but I find it one of the most versatile and veggie/vegan friendly options around. I love to experiment with its texture and the different flavours that can be added to the mix. In this recipe the sesame seeds give a crunch to each bite and add a load of healthy fats to the equation which help long term with skin health, lowering blood pressure and aid digestion. Serve these tasty nuggets with rice, noodles or on top of a salad.

800g firm tofu, drained

5 tbsp white sesame seeds

5 tbsp black sesame seeds

4 tbsp cornflour

Sea salt and freshly ground black pepper

To serve

1 tbsp toasted sesame oil

3 spring onions, finely sliced

Salad or vegetables (green beans and broccoli work well)

Rice or noodles

Gently wrap the drained tofu in a clean tea towel. Place it on a board and balance another board or heavy plate on top. Set aside for 10 minutes, to drain.

Meanwhile, put the white and black sesame seeds in a bowl and combine with the cornflour.

Gently unwrap the tofu and cut it into 1cm thick slices. Season both sides of each slice with salt and pepper, then coat in the sesame seed mixture and set aside.

Put 3 tablespoons of sunflower oil into a non-stick pan and set over a medium heat. Add the coated tofu slices, in batches, and fry for about 3-4 minutes on each side until crisp and golden. Remove and drain on kitchen paper, and keep warm in a low oven. Continue with the remaining tofu, adding in more sunflower oil as needed.

Serve the tofu with the toasted sesame oil drizzled, alongside salad or vegetables and rice or noodles.

CHARRED AUBERGINE WITH TAHINI AND HERBS

SERVES 4, AS A SIDE

Aubergine has such a naturally smoky and rich flavour that often you needn't do much to bring it to life. This is a very simple yet moreish recipe that I think you'll love. It's a great addition to a table packed with dishes of varying vegetables and grains and is full of flavour. The lemon and mint really punch out the flavours and make this is a very fresh and zingy dish.

2 large aubergines

120ml olive oil

4 garlic cloves, crushed

4 tbsp tahini

Small handful of flat leaf parsley, leaves only, finely chopped

Small handful of mint, leaves only, finely chopped

Zest of 1 lemon

Sea salt and freshly ground black pepper

Preheat the grill to medium. Cut the aubergines in half, lengthways, leaving the stalks on. Place skin side down on a baking tray and deeply score the flesh, taking care not to cut through the skin. Drizzle 1 tablespoon olive oil over each aubergine half and rub it into the flesh. Season and cook under the grill for 15 minutes, until golden, then flip over and cook for another 15 minutes until tender.

Remove the aubergine and turn flesh side up again. Combine the crushed garlic with the remaining olive oil and brush over the aubergine flesh. Return to the grill for 5 minutes, until beginning to char, then cover with foil and cook for a final 10 minutes.

Carefully transfer the aubergine halves to a large serving dish. Season, then spoon over the tahini and scatter over the parsley, mint and lemon zest. Serve immediately.

SPICY BEAN STEW

SERVES 4

Getting enough protein is integral to any diet but especially when the decision has been made to reduce or cut out animal products altogether. Beans are a sure fire way of knowing we are getting good protein, essential fibre and also antioxidants. You can easily whack them in casseroles, stews and even bakes and this particular dish is an easy way to feed the masses with the inclusion of those clever beans. I've chosen kidney and butter beans in this stew but really you can add any cans of beans you have in your cupboard. A great help-yourself pot of flavour and good times. Stir in or sprinkle over grated or pulled apart mozzarella, just before serving, if you're not 100 per cent a vegan.

2 tsp coconut oil

1 onion, finely chopped

4 garlic cloves, sliced

1 sweet potato, cut into
   2cm cubes

400g tin chopped tomatoes

500ml vegetable stock

400g tin kidney beans,
   drained and rinsed

400g tin butter beans,
   drained and rinsed

2 tsp sweet smoked paprika

1 tbsp wholegrain mustard

1 tbsp harissa

100g spinach

Sea salt and freshly ground
   black pepper

To serve
Sourdough bread
Extra virgin olive oil

Put the coconut oil into a large pan with the onion and sauté over a medium-high heat for 8 minutes until translucent. Add the garlic and fry for 2 minutes until aromatic. Add the sweet potato, chopped tomatoes, stock, beans, paprika, mustard, harissa and 1 teaspoon of salt and bring to a boil. Reduce the heat and simmer for 25-30 minutes until the potato is very soft and the sauce has thickened.

Stir in the spinach and cook for another few minutes until wilted. Taste and adjust the seasoning.

Serve with wedges of crusty sourdough bread and extra virgin olive oil drizzled over.

SAUSAGE SATAY SKEWERS

SERVES 4

Tofu sausages are one of the few vegan savoury foods my son Rex will eat so this is the perfect little meat-free meal for him. Kids also usually love the novelty of eating something off a skewer. Rex thinks they're very fancy so I've been known to thread prawn toast, waffles and fruit on to them for him on special occasions. What ever gets them eating, eh?! Satay sauce is also a fave in this house – this recipe is refined sugar free and offers up some protein and good fats with the peanut butter.

For the sauce
2 garlic cloves, crushed
½ tsp dried chilli flakes
1 tbsp vegetable oil
2 tsp toasted sesame oil
3 tbsp coconut cream
1 tbsp coconut palm sugar
1 tbsp soy sauce
Zest of 1 lime and 1 tbsp lime juice
3 tbsp crunchy peanut butter
Sea salt and freshly ground black pepper

For the sausages
8 tofu sausages, cut into 3cm pieces
1 tbsp sesame seeds
2 spring onions, finely chopped
Handful of coriander, leaves only
1 red chilli, finely sliced, to serve

Special equipment needed
4 bamboo skewers

Soak the bamboo skewers in cold water, until ready to use. Preheat the oven to 220°C/200°C fan/450°F/gas mark 8. Line a baking tray with baking parchment.

For the satay sauce, put all the ingredients into a food processor or blender and pulse until just combined. If you don't have either of these, crush the garlic and mix the rest by hand. Season to taste.

Place the sausage pieces in a bowl and pour the sauce over. Stir the sausages and sauce together until well coated. Drain the skewers. Thread the sausage pieces onto the skewers and reserve any remaining satay sauce in the bowl. Transfer to the tray and bake for 15 minutes until dry and beginning to colour.

Transfer the skewers to plates, drizzle over the remaining satay sauce and cover with the sesame seeds, coriander and chilli. Serve immediately.

BLACK BEAN AND TOMATO SWEET POTATOES

SERVES 4

Often we stuff peppers and tomatoes but the old sweet potato gets forgotten and is usually just mashed. These little dreamboats are perfect as finger food: mess is encouraged as you won't be able to stop resist taking huge juicy bites! They remind me of a time Reggie Yates and I visited mid-west America for a TV show and we were treated to spicy beans by a camp fire. These hot, flamey flavours will really get you going.

4 large sweet potatoes, halved lengthways

3 tbsp olive oil

200g cherry tomatoes, halved

1 onion, finely chopped

2cm piece of fresh ginger, peeled and grated

3 garlic cloves, crushed

400g tin black beans, drained

200ml vegetable stock

Handful of basil, leaves only

Extra virgin olive oil, for drizzling

Sea salt and freshly ground black pepper

For the tahini dressing
4 tbsp tahini

200g soya milk yoghurt

1 garlic clove, crushed

½ tsp sweet smoked paprika

½ tsp dried chilli flakes

Preheat the oven to 220°C/200°C fan/450°F/gas mark 8.

Coat the potato halves with half the olive oil. Season generously and place on a baking tray. Bake for 30-40 minutes, depending on the size of the potatoes, until the flesh is soft and buttery and the skin is crisp.

Meanwhile, heat the remaining oil in a pan over a medium heat. Add the tomatoes and fry for 4-5 minutes until blistered. Remove and set aside. Add in the onion, ginger and garlic and sauté for 8 minutes until softened, taking care not to let them burn. Add the black beans, tomatoes and vegetable stock and bring to a boil. Reduce the heat and simmer until almost all of the stock has evaporated off. Season well, to taste.

In a bowl, combine together the dressing ingredients and season to taste.

Place the sweet potato halves on plates and spoon the black bean mixture and tomatoes over. Dollop over the dressing and scatter over the basil. Drizzle with a little extra virgin olive oil and serve immediately.

CHARRED SPICED CAULIFLOWER WITH SPRING ONIONS AND SESAME SEEDS

SERVES 4, AS A SIDE

This is a perfect sharing platter if you're planning on having people over and lots of big dishes out for people to choose and scoop from. It's a warming, comforting dish with caramel tones and loads of zing from the ginger. It's quick and easy to make and gives cauliflower another string to its bow.

400g cauliflower, broken into small florets

80g non-dairy yoghurt

1 tbsp harissa

1 tbsp toasted sesame oil

1 tbsp soy sauce

3cm piece of fresh ginger, peeled and finely grated

1 tbsp coconut palm sugar

3 garlic cloves, crushed

2 spring onions, finely sliced

2 tsp sesame seeds, roasted

Sea salt and freshly ground black pepper

Bring a large pan of salted water to the boil and cook the cauliflower florets for 2 minutes, until tender but not falling apart. Drain well, pat dry with kitchen paper and set aside.

In a bowl combine together the remaining ingredients, apart from the spring onions and sesame seeds. Add the cauliflower and toss gently to coat. Season with a little salt and pepper.

Place a griddle pan over a medium-high heat. Cook the cauliflower, in batches, turning now and again, for 5-6 minutes, until tender and slightly blackened and charred in places. Keep warm in a low oven until all the cauliflower is cooked.

Serve with the spring onions and sesame seeds scattered over.

SWEET POTATO DUMPLING TOPPED VEGETABLE PIE

SERVES 4

The bottom tofu layer of this dish is similar to that of a dumpling filling and it's topped with light fluffy sweet potato. It's so hearty and comforting and makes for the perfect Sunday lunch option or a warming dinner on a cold, blustery night.

2 tbsp coconut oil

1 carrot, finely chopped

1 celery stalk, finely chopped

1 leek, finely chopped

3 garlic cloves, crushed

400g firm tofu, drained and cut into small pieces

200g tin sweetcorn, rinsed and drained

200g frozen peas

400g tin chopped tomatoes

½ tsp ground cumin

½ tsp sweet smoked paprika

3 tbsp soy sauce

2 tbsp balsamic vinegar

400ml coconut cream

Large handful of flat leaf parsley, leaves only, roughly chopped

3 large sweet potatoes, roughly chopped

100g white spelt flour, sifted

Olive oil, for drizzling

Sea salt and freshly ground black pepper

Put the coconut oil into a large pan and set over a medium-high heat. Add the carrot, celery and leek and sauté for 8 minutes, stirring frequently, until softened but not browned. Add the garlic and cook for another 2-3 minutes until aromatic. Add the tofu, sweetcorn, peas, chopped tomatoes, cumin, paprika, 2 tablespoons of soy sauce, balsamic vinegar and all but 2 tablespoons of the coconut cream. Bring to a boil, then reduce the heat and simmer for 20 minutes. Stir through most of the parsley and season to taste.

Meanwhile, bring a large pan of salted water to the boil and cook the sweet potatoes for 15 minutes or until tender. Drain thoroughly and mash with the remaining coconut cream and remaining soy sauce. Season to taste.

Preheat the oven to 220°C/200°C fan/450°F/gas mark 8.

Transfer the tofu and vegetable mixture to a medium casserole dish and top with large spoonfuls of the sweet potato mash. Drizzle over some olive oil and bake for 15-20 minutes until golden and slightly charred. Remove, scatter over the remaining parsley and serve immediately.

Parties for me have changed drastically over the last decade. I've always adored hosting and having house parties as I'm a home body, so the option of walking up the stairs to my bedroom rather than having to endure a 40 minute cab ride home at an unthinkable hour or run for the last train, is pure joy.

In my twenties I invited friends, friends of friends, and friends of those friends in to dance wildly on my sofas, drink sloppily made cocktails and subsequently drop phones accidentally down the loo. Wonderful mayhem which involved very little food. The house parties have continued into the next decade of my life but with a lovely twist. They're in the daytime and are ALL about food. Making party food is pure joy as you can be that bit more decadent, that jot more daring and a lot more fun. Whether it's one of my kid's birthdays, an Easter egg hunt for the kids in the school holidays or simply for the heck of it I love to get my most favourite people over for a good old feed up.

Party food is traditionally very un-vegan and pretty unhealthy – perhaps historically seen as foods doused in sugar, lathered in fat and showered in salt. The party foods I have concocted in this chapter are 100 per cent vegan, refined sugar free and full of the good stuff needed to boost our energy levels and keep us topped up with fibre, vitamins and protein. Oh, and they happen to be pretty fun too! Fun to make and really fun to eat. I love Halloween for the kids as they love to dress up and make foolish treats. Honey loves the Chocolate Halloween spiders (page 178) so much that we end up eating them pretty much all year round! The vegan Mince pies (page 182) are a favourite of mine as I revel in all things Christmas; the flavours, smells and cosiness of it make me tingle with joy. Celebrate all year round with these vegan wonders!

PARTY
Time

BBQ BROCCOLI BITES

SERVES 4, AS A SIDE

I made these for a mixed bunch of family and friends recently and they went down a treat. Sometimes I worry about serving vegan options to hard-core meat-eaters but these were gobbled up with glee. They're also easy to prepare which I think is important for party food as you want to be enjoying yourself rather than constantly standing over the oven. Whack them in the oven, then party time.

120g white spelt flour

1 tsp chilli powder

1 tsp sweet smoked paprika

1 tsp garlic powder

1 tsp onion powder

1 tsp ground cumin

1 tsp salt

400g broccoli, broken into bite-sized florets

200ml BBQ sauce

Small handful of chives, finely chopped

½ tsp sesame seeds

Preheat the oven to 220°C/200°C fan/450°F/gas mark 8. Line a baking tray with baking parchment.

Put the flour, spices and salt into a large bowl and stir to combine. Rinse the broccoli florets and shake off any excess water. Add to the bowl and mix with the spiced flour until thoroughly coated. Shake off any excess flour and transfer to the lined baking tray. Roast for 10 minutes until golden and almost tender.

After 10 minutes, combine the roasted broccoli with the BBQ sauce and stir to coat. Transfer the mixture back to the baking tray and cook the broccoli for a further 10 minutes until sticky and caramelised.

Serve immediately with the chives and sesame seeds scattered over.

NO PIGS IN BLANKETS

SERVES 4, AS A SNACK

◇◇

For those missing this festive treat I thought I would come up with a little alternative using aubergines as the blankets. You can make them with shop-bought vegan sausages or my Black bean sausages (page 126). The tahini maple drizzle really sets these little vegan piggies off perfectly.

1 aubergine, trimmed

3-4 tablespoons olive oil

8 vegan sausages (Black bean sausages, page 126, or shop-bought tofu sausages), halved lengthways

16 sundried tomatoes in oil, drained

2 tbsp tahini

Small handful of flat leaf parsley, leaves only, roughly chopped

2 tbsp pomegranate seeds

Sea salt and freshly ground black pepper

Special equipment needed
Cocktail sticks

Cut the aubergine in half lengthways, and then cut each half into 8 thin slices, again lengthways, from top to bottom. Brush each side with oil and season well. Place a large non-stick frying pan over a medium heat and cook the aubergine slices in batches, for about 4 minutes on each side, until golden and tender. Remove to a plate.

Preheat the oven to 200°C/180°C fan/400°F/gas mark 6.

Wrap each half of tofu sausage with a slice of aubergine and sit a sundried tomato on top. Secure everything together with a cocktail stick and place on a lined baking tray. Roast for 10 minutes then transfer to a serving dish.

Drizzle the tahini over the baked sausages. Scatter the parsley and pomegranate seeds over, to serve.

MOREISH MINI BITES

These are really lovely sweet and salty treats to have in bowls for after dinner or at a party. The brittle is perfect adorn a bowl of vegan ice-cream in sharp beautiful splinters and my family adore popcorn so if we have mates over we'll usually have a big bowl of this on the go in the kitchen throughout the day – enjoy!

NUTTY BRITTLE SERVES 6

150g raw unsalted pistachio nuts, roughly chopped

3 tbsp sesame seeds

2 tbsp chia seeds

3 tbsp raw white quinoa

40g oats

30g coconut palm sugar

¾ tsp sea salt

3 tbsp coconut oil

1 tsp vanilla bean paste

100ml brown rice syrup

Line a baking tray with baking parchment. Preheat the oven to 160°C/140°C fan/325°F/gas mark 3. In a bowl, combine together the pistachio nuts, sesame seeds, chia seeds, quinoa, oats, coconut palm sugar and salt.

Put the coconut oil, vanilla and brown rice syrup into a pan and melt over a low heat. Pour over the dry mixture and combine until everything is thoroughly coated.

Spread the mixture out on the tray with the back of a spoon to a thickness of about ½ a centimetre. Bake for 25-30 minutes until golden. Remove and leave to cool. Once cool, break into shards. Store in an airtight container in the fridge for up to 2 weeks.

MISO CARAMEL POPCORN SERVES 4, AS A SNACK

1 tbsp sunflower oil

100g popcorn kernels

50g maple syrup

80g coconut palm sugar

2 tbsp white miso paste

½ tsp ground cinnamon

¼ tsp bicarbonate of soda

Line a baking tray with baking parchment.

Put the oil in a large pan with a tightly fitting lid and set over a medium-high heat. Add the corn kernels, cover with the lid (to stop any popping corn from escaping!), and cook for 3-4 minutes, shaking the pan frequently, until the corn has stopped popping. Remove from the heat.

Put the maple syrup, coconut palm sugar and miso paste into a small pan and set over a medium-high heat. Stir occasionally to combine and cook for 3-4 minutes until the sugar has mostly dissolved and the mixture has thickened. Stir in the cinnamon and bicarbonate of soda and immediately pour over the popcorn and stir to combine. Transfer to the lined baking tray, spread the coated corn out into a single layer and leave to cool.

SPICED CHOCOLATE AND CASHEW SQUARES

MAKES 20

I put a plate of these out the other weekend as I had three great girlfriends of mine over and without really knowing it, with cups of tea in hand we munched our way through quite a few of these decadent squares. I'm a chocoholic so they give me the hit I need but without a crazy sugar high. The base is full of good oats and nuts for protein and fibre – plus they're fun to make.

For the base

100g blanched hazelnuts

100g oat cakes

150g unsulphured dried apricots

2 tbsp coconut oil, melted

Pinch of sea salt

For the middle layer

350g cashew butter, plus more to drizzle

2 tsp mixed spice

7 tbsp maple syrup

90g coconut oil

For the top layer

200g dark chocolate, minimum 70% cocoa solids, broken into small pieces

2 tbsp coconut oil, melted

Special equipment needed

20 x 26cm cake tin

Line the tin fully with baking parchment.

Add all the base ingredients to a food processor and blitz until the mixture is completely ground down and sticks together when pressed between your fingers. Transfer to the lined tin and press very firmly down to form an even and smooth base. Place in the freezer for 15 minutes to set.

For the middle layer, put all the ingredients into a pan and set over a low heat. Stir until the coconut oil has melted and everything has come together. Pour over the chilled base, smooth out and return to the freezer for 20 minutes to set.

For the top layer, melt the chocolate and coconut oil in a heatproof bowl set over a pan of barely simmering water, ensuring the base of the bowl does not touch the water. Pour the mixture over the middle layer and smooth out. Drizzle over a few teaspoons of cashew nut butter, scatter over a pinch of sea salt and return to the freezer. After 10 minutes, when the chocolate is barely set, score the chocolate with a sharp knife into 20 equal squares, so that the chocolate does not break into shards when you come to cut it later. Cover and refrigerate for 1 hour or until ready to serve.

To serve, cut into squares along the lines you scored earlier. Keep in an airtight container in the fridge for up to 1 week or for up to 3 months in the freezer.

GINGERBREAD PEOPLE

MAKES AROUND 20

My favourite biscuits to make with my kids! They're super easy to make and my kids adore decorating them with funny faces and elaborate buttons when cooled. You may be worried that this biscuit mix is too brittle to pick up or cut with a cookie cutter but it's wonderfully soft and holds together well due to the flaxseeds, which are also ace for the gut.

For the gingerbread
1½ tbsp ground flax seeds
3½ tbsp boiling water
300g white spelt flour plus extra for dusting
150g coconut palm sugar
150g coconut oil, chilled and cut into small pieces
3 tbsp blackstrap molasses or maple syrup
1 tsp baking powder
¼ tsp fine sea salt
2 tsp vanilla extract
2 tsp ground ginger
1 tsp ground cinnamon
½ tsp mixed spice

For the icing
150g icing sugar, sifted
1½ tbsp non-dairy milk or water

Special equipment needed
Gingerbread men cutters
Piping bag and writing nozzle or a resealable plastic food bag

Preheat the oven to 180°C/160°C fan/350°F/gas mark 4. Line 2 baking trays with baking parchment.

Combine the flax seeds and water in a small bowl and set aside, for 3 minutes, to thicken.

Put the flour, sugar and coconut oil into a food processor and blitz until the mixture resembles very fine breadcrumbs. Transfer to a bowl and stir in the molasses, baking powder, salt, vanilla, ginger, cinnamon, mixed spice and flax seed mixture until it comes together. Knead briefly to form a ball of dough, adding in a few drops of water if it is a little dry.

Dust your work surface with plenty of flour and roll out the dough to a thickness of 5mm. Cut out the gingerbread people and carefully transfer to the lined baking trays. Dip your cutter in flour each time if it is sticking.

Bake the biscuits for 10-12 minutes, until they are a shade darker and slightly firm to the touch. Remove and leave to cool on the trays for a few minutes before gently transferring to a wire cooling rack to cool completely.

Meanwhile, combine together the icing sugar and non-dairy milk or water, stirring until you have a very thick and sticky icing. Transfer the icing into a piping bag fitted with the nozzle or into a resealable plastic food bag with the very tip of one of the corners snipped off. Pipe faces and buttons onto the cold biscuits and leave to set. Store in an airtight container for up to 1 week.

CHOCOLATE HALLOWEEN SPIDERS

SERVES 18–20 BALLS

My daughter Honey loves chocolate energy balls so we always have some in an airtight container in the fridge. They're the perfect sweet treat for kids as they won't make them hyper and they also have a lot of gut boosting fibre in them. This recipe makes up a batch of delicious balls that act as the spider's body which you can then decorate however you please. Add liquorice legs and fruit for eyes or any other fun alternatives you find.

For the balls
10 Medjool dates, pitted
80g whole almonds
1½ tbsp coconut oil
1 tbsp almond butter
1 tbsp chia seeds
1 tbsp raw cacao powder or cocoa powder

To decorate
Thin liquorice strips, for the legs
Freeze dried raspberry pieces or small white chocolate balls, for the eyes

Blitz together all the ball ingredients in a food processor until they come together when pressed between your fingers.

Shape the mixture into 18-20 oblong balls, roughly 1 heaped teaspoon per ball. Use short strips of liquorice to create the legs, pushing 4 pieces into each side of the ball. For the eyes, gently press 2 pieces of freeze dried raspberry or white chocolate balls into the surface. Serve immediately or store in an airtight container in the fridge for up to a week.

FESTIVE CHOCOLATE ALMOND LOAF

MAKES 1 LOAF

I saw a Christmas recipe last December for a festive choc loaf and loved the idea, so set about making a vegan version. The grated apples seem to do the trick in keeping this loaf well held together and the dried apricots give it so much chew and a load of flavour. The chai tea works so well with the cacao and the spices make you instantly feel Christmassy. It's a lovely afternoon treat for neighbours popping in and the leftovers make a pretty gorgeous breakfast, too.

800ml boiling water

2 chai teabags

500g unsulphured dried apricots, roughly chopped

2 apples, peeled, cored and grated

Zest of 1 orange

200g almonds, roughly chopped

4 tbsp raw cacao powder or cocoa powder, sifted

4 tbsp maple syrup

1 tsp ground cinnamon

1 tsp ground nutmeg

Pinch of salt

320g white spelt flour, sifted

1 tsp baking powder

Coconut oil, vegan spread or jam, to serve (optional)

Special equipment needed
900g loaf tin

Preheat the oven to 200°C/180°C fan/400°F/gas mark 6. Grease the loaf tin with a flavourless oil and line fully with baking parchment.

Pour the boiling water over the teabags and leave for 2 minutes.

Put the chopped dried apricots and grated apple in a saucepan and cover with the hot chai tea. Bring to a boil, then reduce the heat and simmer for 15 minutes. Remove from the heat and leave to cool for 5 minutes, then drain off as much liquid as possible. Transfer the cooked drained apricots and apple to a food processor and blitz until smooth.

Place the blitzed fruit in a bowl and add the remaining ingredients. Beat until thoroughly combined. Press the mixture into the prepared tin and bake for 60 minutes until deep golden brown and firm. If the top is browning too quickly, cover with foil.

Remove and leave to cool for 15 minutes, then transfer to a wire cooling rack to cool completely. Serve sliced as it is or with some coconut oil, vegan spread or jam.

MINCE PIES

MAKES 18

My lovely friend Tanya has a café in London that makes the most exceptional vegan mince pies which each year I seem to inhale at an alarming rate. This recipe is inspired by Tanya's but is booze-free in honour of my sober husband. You may never eat a regular mince pie again!

For the pastry
270g white spelt flour plus extra for dusting
250g coconut oil, chilled and cut into small pieces
¼ tsp salt
Zest of 1 orange
70ml iced water
60ml maple syrup
Soya milk and maple syrup, for glazing
Icing sugar, to dust (optional)

For the filling
80g sultanas
80g raisins
80g currant
80g mixed peel
25g pecans, finely chopped
100g coconut palm sugar
½ tsp mixed spice
1 tbsp coconut oil, melted
Zest of ½ lemon
1 tbsp orange juice
1 cooking apple, unpeeled, cored and grated

Special equipment needed
2 x 9 hole muffin tins
9-10cm round cutter
Smaller round or star cutter

For the pastry, put the flour, coconut oil, salt and half the orange zest into a food processor and pulse on and off until the mixture resembles fine breadcrumbs. Transfer to a bowl and stir through the iced water and maple syrup. Use your hand to gather the dough into a ball. Flatten, wrap in clingfilm and refrigerate for 20 minutes.

Meanwhile, in a large bowl place all the filling ingredients plus the remaining orange zest and stir well.

Preheat the oven to 190°C/170°C fan/375°F/gas mark 5. Grease the muffin tins with a flavourless oil or vegan butter.

Roll out the dough to a thickness of 3mm. Use the larger round cutter to stamp out 18 circles. Gently press them into the muffin tins and spoon 1½ tablespoons of filling into each case. Cut out 18 smaller circles or stars and place on top. Whisk together 1 tablespoon each of soya milk and maple syrup and brush over the top of the mince pies, to glaze.

Bake the pies for 25-30 minutes or until they turn deep golden. Remove and leave to cool for 10 minutes in the tins, then transfer to a wire cooling rack to cool completely. Serve with a little dusting of icing sugar, if you like. These will keep in an airtight container for up to 3 days or can be frozen for up to a month.

VIRGIN COCKTAILS

As the years have passed and my life has changed shape I have naturally leaned more towards eating a well-balanced diet and I find I'm not drinking very much at all anymore. I have the odd drink if I'm out with mates or at a wedding, but the days where I drink myself into oblivion are over. My husband is completely sober so I think it's always nice to offer up some booze-free drinks when you're throwing a party. Of course if you love the odd drink you can add a splash of voddy or gin to the mix as well as non-alcoholic spirits such as Seedlip. The Espresso notini (below) is my absolute fave!

ESPRESSO NOTINI

SERVES 2

100ml chilled espresso coffee (either from granules and water, cooled and then refrigerated or shop-bought iced coffee)
100ml Seedlip Spice 94
2 tbsp maple syrup
Ice

Mix the espresso, Seedlip Spice 94 and maple syrup thoroughly in a jug with some ice or, if you have one, shake vigorously in a cocktail shaker over ice and then strain into two chilled glasses. Serve with more ice, if you like.

ICED LEMON MINT SPRITZ

SERVES 4

500ml boiling water

2 mint tea bags

4 tbsp maple syrup

Zest of 3 limes and 2 tbsp
  lime juice

Juice of 2 lemons

To serve
Small bunch of mint

Sparkling water

Ice

Pour the boiling water over the mint tea bags and allow to brew for 2 minutes. Remove the tea bags and allow the tea to cool. Once cool transfer to the fridge to chill. In a jug, combine together the chilled mint tea, maple syrup, lime zest and juice and lemon juice.

Rub a few mint sprigs between your hands and place inside each glass. Divide the mint tea mixture between the glasses and top up with sparkling water and ice. Serve immediately.

POMEGRANATE BOMB

SERVES 2

400ml pomegranate juice

1 tbsp pomegranate
  molasses

100ml freshly squeezed
  orange juice

Ice

2 strips of orange peel

Mix the pomegranate juice, molasses and orange juice thoroughly over ice or, if you have one, shake vigorously in a cocktail shaker over ice and then strain into two chilled glasses filled with ice. Twist the orange peel to release the oils and sit it in the top of the drink. Serve immediately.

I have baked and made desserts for as long as I can remember, but I have only recently mastered vegan baking. I would, age 6, make little gooey jam tarts packed with butter with my nan Ruby, or Victoria sponges oozing tidal waves of cream out the sides when I moved in to my first flat, and more recently chocolate birthday cakes for my kids piled high with creamy icing. I was nervous to step in to the new world of vegan baking as what I had been doing for years seemed to work and had become habitual.

Vegan baking can appear very complicated with the lack of eggs and butter but actually it's very simple once you make a few switches. I've found, since diving headfirst into the world of vegan baking, that you can create fluffy cloud-like cakes without a single egg and can perfect the most glossy chocolate brownies minus the huge block of butter.

Vegan baking also lends itself to using more interesting and slightly out-of-the-box ingredients. So, I'm no stranger to whacking a tin of pulses into a traybake or a cooked beetroot into a brownie. There are so many benefits to baking in this way as you of course get that extra hit of veg and protein in something that normally would be a purely decadent treat.

I'm not the sort of person who can eat a savoury main course and then move onto the next thing in my day. I need that sweet full stop. That little hit of endorphins crated by a smidge of chocolate cake or nibble of ice-cream. I feel hard done by if I don't get my hit so my challenge throughout my thirties was how to make those 'sweet something's' nutritious. It has become a mission and a passion as I whip up cakes on a near daily basis for those much needed after school snacks for my kids and for my aforementioned post-meal needs.

Creating vegan bakes has taken my baking into new dimensions and I hope you find the recipes in this chapter as enjoyable as I do. Whether it's the Tahini fudge brownies (page 194) which are so gooey and rich in flavour you'll find it hard to stop! Or the Blueberry and cannellini bean tray bake (page 197) which offers up some unexpected protein and juicy, fruity flavour. Ditch the eggs and watch these bakes blow your mind. Happy baking!

the
sweetest
thing

CHOCOLATE ORANGE MOUSSE

SERVES 4

Sometimes the alchemy of cooking blows my mind and making chocolate mousse is the perfect example of why. It feels like a little science experiment making this vegan dessert as you watch the chocolate thicken up and take form. Chocolate orange is one of my favourite childhood flavours as my great nan Cotton used to always give us kids a chocolate orange – she seemed to have piles of them on top of her cabinets waiting for us. This luxurious dessert will not disappoint.

100ml chilled water

Zest of ½ orange and 3 tbsp orange juice

200g dark chocolate, minimum 70% cocoa solids, broken into small pieces

Ice cubes

150g mixed berries, fresh if possible

1 tbsp desiccated coconut, toasted

Put the water, orange zest and juice into a heatproof bowl oven a pan of simmering water set over a low heat. Add the chocolate and stir constantly until the chocolate has melted and the mixture has come together.

Take the bowl off the pan and position it inside a larger bowl partly filled with the ice cubes and water. Whisk the mixture continuously until it has cooled and become thick and voluminous. Take care not to cool it too much as the mixture will go grainy. If this does happen, simply melt it again and repeat the process.

Divide the mixture between 4 small glasses or ramekin dishes and refrigerate for at least 1 hour until set and well chilled.

If using strawberries, remove the stems and cores and cut into bite-size pieces, then serve the mousse with the mixed berries and desiccated coconut scattered over.

POMEGRANATE AND YOGHURT CAKE

MAKES 1 X 23CM ROUND CAKE

SERVES 8–10

If you're looking for a moist cake, you've come to the right place. The coconut yoghurt gives this cake some seriously mouth-watering bounce while the lemon and pomegranate seeds boost the juice factor. It's easy to make too!

3 tbsp ground flax seeds

8 tbsp boiling water

170g coconut oil, softened

190g coconut palm sugar

250g coconut yoghurt

150g white spelt flour, sifted

100g ground almonds

1 tsp baking powder

1 tsp bicarbonate of soda

1 lemon, zested and 1 tbsp juice

3 tbsp oat milk

1 pomegranate

Special equipment needed
23cm round springform tin

Preheat the oven to 170°C/150°C fan/gas mark 3. Grease the tin with a flavourless oil and line fully.

Put the ground flax seeds into a bowl with the water and set aside for 3 minutes.

With an electric whisk, beat together the coconut oil and sugar for up to 5 minutes, until light and creamy. Slowly beat in the flax seed mixture, 120g of the coconut yoghurt and all the remaining ingredients, apart from the pomegranate. The batter should be thick, but still loose enough to fall off a wooden spoon (if not, add in another tablespoon or two of the oat milk). Transfer to the lined tin and bake for 40-45 minutes, until a skewer inserted into the centre comes out clean. If it is browning too quickly, cover with foil. Remove from the oven and leave to cool for 10 minutes, then turn out onto a wire rack to cool completely.

Cut the pomegranate in half and with the back of a wooden spoon, bash the seeds out of the skin into a large bowl, catching all the juice as well. Pick out any pith and discard then drain the pomegranate seeds through a sieve, catching the juice in another bowl. Combine 2 tablespoons of the juice with the remaining yoghurt to create a light pink yoghurt drizzle. Once the cake is cool, position on a serving plate, spoon the yoghurt over the top and spread it out, allowing it to drip down over the sides. Scatter the pomegranate seeds over the top and serve immediately.

TAHINI FUDGE BROWNIES

MAKES 16 SQUARES

Tahini is such a dream when you're making vegan bakes. It is so creamy and packed with good fats and protein and it has a very distinct exotic flavour. These brownies rival any non-vegan kind as they're unbelievably gooey and soft. Warning, they won't last long with hungry mouths around!

2 tbsp ground flax seeds

6 tbsp boiling water

200g dark chocolate, minimum 70% cocoa solids, broken into small pieces

100g coconut oil

130g white spelt flour

40g raw cacao powder or cocoa powder

½ tsp baking powder

¼ tsp fine sea salt

170g coconut palm sugar

125g tahini plus 3 tbsp to decorate

Special equipment needed
16 x 24cm cake tin

Preheat the oven to 180°C/160°C fan/350°F/gas mark 4. Line the tin fully with baking parchment.

Combine the flax seeds and water in a small bowl and set aside for 5 minutes until thick and gloopy.

Place the chocolate and coconut oil in a heatproof bowl. Place the bowl over a pan of barely simmering water, ensuring the base of the bowl does not come into contact with the water. Stir now and again until the chocolate and coconut oil have melted and come together.

Sift the flour, cacao powder and baking powder into a bowl, then stir in the salt and coconut sugar. Add the melted chocolate and coconut oil, the flax seed mixture and tahini and stir until thoroughly combined.

Transfer to the lined tin and use the back of a spoon to level the surface. Drizzle over the remaining 3 tablespoons of tahini. Bake for about 20-25 minutes, until barely set with a little wobble in the centre. Leave to cool completely, then remove and cut into 16 squares. Keep in an airtight container for up to 5 days.

BLUEBERRY AND CANNELLINI BEAN TRAY BAKE

MAKES 16 SQUARES

Call me cruel, but I love to trick my kids into eating good stuff without them knowing it. This cake is a good example as it holds two tins of protein-packed beans within it but simply tastes likes a dreamy blueberry cake. It's so easy to make and lovely cut into slices and served with the drizzle on top. More beans equals more protein, better gut health and a really interesting way of baking.

For the icing
60g tahini
3 tbsp maple syrup
2 tbsp coconut oil, melted
150g coconut milk yoghurt

For the cake
2 x 400g tins cannellini
   beans, rinsed and drained
5 tbsp maple syrup
75g coconut palm sugar
1 tsp vanilla extract
100ml light olive oil or
   sunflower oil
80ml oat milk
Zest of 1 lemon and 2 tbsp
   lemon juice
150g white spelt flour, sifted
2 tsp baking powder
Pinch of sea salt
150g blueberries

Special equipment needed
16 x 24cm cake tin

Preheat the oven to 200°C/180°C fan/400°F/gas mark 6. Grease the cake tin with a flavourless oil and line it fully.

For the icing, mix together the tahini, maple syrup and melted coconut oil until thoroughly combined. Stir in the yoghurt, cover and refrigerate until needed.

For the cake, put the cannellini beans, maple syrup, sugar, vanilla, oil, milk and lemon zest and juice into a food processor and blitz until smooth. Transfer to a large bowl and fold in the flour, baking powder and salt. Pour into the lined tin and scatter over half the blueberries. Bake for 25-30 minutes, until a skewer inserted into the centre comes out mostly clean. Remove and leave to cool in the tin for 10 minutes, then transfer to a wire cooling rack to cool completely.

When ready to serve, place the tray bake on a serving board, whisk the icing and spread over the top. Scatter over the remaining blueberries and serve cut into squares. Keep in an airtight container in the fridge for up to 2 days.

BANANA, AVOCADO AND CHOCOLATE LOAF

MAKES 1 LOAF

In one of our local cafés they always have cakes on the counter and this combination of flavours is regularly on display. I had never seen avocado used in cakes before so I have them to thank for inspiring me to create this yummy number.

2 tbsp ground flax seeds

6 tbsp boiling water

125g coconut oil, at room temperature

125g coconut palm sugar

2 very ripe bananas, peeled and mashed

1 ripe avocado, halved, stoned and mashed

4 tbsp almond or rice milk

150g white spelt flour

2 tbsp raw cacao powder or cocoa powder

½ tsp fine sea salt

2 tsp baking powder

60g dark chocolate, minimum 70% cocoa solids, broken into small pieces (optional)

2 tbsp roasted flaked almonds (optional)

Special equipment needed
900g loaf tin

Preheat the oven to 180°C/160°C fan/350°F/gas mark 4. Grease the loaf tin with a flavourless oil and line fully with baking parchment.

Combine the flax seeds and water in a small bowl and set aside for at least 3 minutes.

In a large bowl cream together the coconut oil and sugar until light and fluffy, an electric whisk is useful for this. Beat in the bananas, avocado, milk and flax seed mixture, until well combined.

In another bowl combine together the flour, cacao powder, salt and baking powder. Gradually add this into the wet mixture, until it has just come together. Don't over mix as it will make the loaf tough.

Transfer the mixture to the lined loaf tin and bake for 45-50 minutes, until an inserted skewer comes out clean. If the top is browning too quickly, cover with foil. Remove and leave to cool in the tin for 10 minutes, then turn out onto a wire cooling rack to cool completely.

If you want to top the cooled loaf with chocolate and nuts, place the chocolate in a small heatproof bowl over a pan of barely simmering water, ensuring the base of the bowl does not come into contact with the water. Stir now and again until the chocolate has melted. Drizzle the chocolate over the loaf and sprinkle the nuts on top. Allow to set before serving. Keep for up to 2 days in an airtight container.

UPSIDE DOWN PLUM CAKE

SERVES 8–10

I love an upside down cake as they feel quite old school. They always look pretty without much effort as the fruit is doing all the talking – and here the fruit is doing all the walking too as cooking releases their full, rich flavours. Plums sometimes get forgotten and overshadowed by the sweeter and more tropical fruits like mango or those branded 'superfoods' like blueberries. Poor plums. They're full of antioxidants and great for good gut health and make this cake a tangy, yet sweet, treat.

2 tbsp ground flax seeds

5 tbsp boiling water

150g coconut oil, melted

250g coconut palm sugar

6 plums, halved and stoned

170g white spelt flour

120g coconut milk yoghurt
plus extra to serve

2 tsp baking powder

Special equipment needed
20cm deep round cake tin

Preheat the oven to 180°C/160°C fan/350°F/gas mark 4. Grease the tin with a flavourless oil and line fully.

Combine the flax seeds and water in a small bowl and set aside for 3 minutes.

Drizzle 2 tablespoons of the melted coconut oil over the base of the cake tin, then evenly scatter over 50g of the coconut palm sugar. Cut the halved plums into 1cm wedges and arrange them in the base of the tin in a fan-like pattern.

Put the remaining coconut oil and sugar into a bowl with the flax seed mixture. Add the flour, yoghurt and baking powder and fold together. Pour over the plums and bake for 40-45 minutes, until an inserted skewer comes out clean. Leave to cool in the tin for 10 minutes, then carefully invert the cake onto a wire cooling rack to cool completely. Serve with more yoghurt.

DOUGHNUT BALLS WITH CHOCOLATE AND DATE SAUCE

MAKES 20

My son Rex is obsessed with doughnuts and we've had a lot of fun and failed attempts at making the perfect batch at home. Home baked or cooked foods will always taste better and this is one of Rex's absolute favourites. Although it is best to eat these as an occasional treat!

For the doughnuts
260g white spelt flour plus extra for dusting
2 tsp baking powder
60g coconut palm sugar
½ tsp fine sea salt
120ml soya milk
65g vegan margarine, melted
1 litre sunflower oil, for deep frying

For the sauce
60g dark chocolate, minimum 70% cocoa solids, broken into small pieces
2 tbsp coconut oil
4 tbsp date syrup

Special equipment needed
Medium heavy-based pan for deep frying

Put the flour, baking powder, sugar and salt into a large bowl and stir in the milk and melted vegan margarine until it comes together into a wet dough. Scrape the dough out of the bowl onto a board dusted with plenty of flour. Roll the dough in the flour so it is no longer sticky, divide into 20 pieces of equal size and roll into balls.

Pour the sunflower oil into a medium heavy-based pan. Heat the oil to 180°C – use a sugar thermometer to check the temperature. Otherwise, test cook a small piece of the dough: it should turn golden and rise to the surface within 1 minute when the oil is ready. Take great care when cooking with hot oil and never leave it unattended.

Once the oil is ready, very gently lower 3 doughnut balls into the oil and fry until puffed and golden, about 3-4 minutes, turning now and again. Remove using a slotted spoon and place on a plate lined with kitchen paper. Repeat to cook the remaining doughnuts.

For the sauce, place the chocolate and coconut oil in a heatproof bowl. Place the bowl over a pan of barely simmering water, ensuring the base of the bowl does not come into contact with the water. Stir now and again until the chocolate and coconut oil have melted and come together. Stir the date syrup into the melted chocolate and coconut oil.

Pile the doughnut balls onto a serving plate and drizzle over the chocolate and date sauce. Serve immediately.

BANANA AND ALMOND BUTTER COOKIES

MAKES 20 COOKIES

A firm favourite in our house. Every member of the family approves, which always helps, so a batch can easily be gobbled up within a couple of days. Packed with protein from the nut butter and held together perfectly by the banana, these little cookies are a no-fuss, quick and easy recipe you'll go back to again and again.

200g white spelt flour, sifted

100g coconut palm sugar

2 tbsp raw cacao powder or cocoa powder

½ tsp baking powder

Pinch of sea salt

70g coconut oil, melted

1 banana, peeled and mashed

2 tbsp almond butter

Preheat the oven to 200°C/180°C fan/400°F/gas mark 6. Line two baking trays with baking parchment.

In a bowl combine together the flour, sugar, cacao powder, baking powder and salt.

In a separate bowl beat the melted coconut oil together with the mashed banana and almond butter. Add to the dry ingredients and combine together.

Take 1½ tablespoons of the mixture, roll into a ball and then slightly flatten. Place on the lined baking tray and repeat with the remaining dough, leaving a little space between each cookie. Bake for 10-12 minutes, until dry around the edges. Remove and leave to cool on the tray for 15 minutes before transferring to a wire cooling rack to cool completely. Keep in an airtight container for up to 3 days or frozen for up to a month.

CHOCOLATE FUDGE CAKE

MAKES 1 X 20CM ROUND CAKE

Need I say more? Chocolate, fudge and cake in the same sentence and the promise of it all being completely vegan. This is the cake I make the most at home as the kids adore it. The apple cider vinegar almost acts as the eggs as it helps bind the mixture together without any of its flavour coming thorough. It's rich, mega chocolatey and so, so light!

6 Medjool dates, pitted

250ml non-dairy milk

1 tsp apple cider vinegar

160g coconut palm sugar

70g coconut oil, melted

1 tsp vanilla extract

120g white spelt flour, sifted

50g raw cacao powder or cocoa powder

½ tsp baking powder

½ tsp bicarbonate of soda

1 tbsp almond butter

Pinch of fine sea salt

50g dark chocolate, minimum 70% cocoa solids, broken into small pieces (optional)

Non-dairy yoghurt or ice cream, to serve

Special equipment needed
20cm round springform tin

Preheat the oven to 180°C/160°C fan/350°F/gas mark 4. Grease the tin with a flavourless oil and line fully.

Put the dates into a bowl and cover with warm water. Set aside for 20 minutes.

In a large bowl, whisk together the milk, vinegar, sugar, coconut oil, vanilla, flour, cacao powder, baking powder and bicarbonate of soda, until free of lumps.

Drain the dates, reserving 1 tablespoon of the soaking liquid, and transfer to a food processor with the almond butter and a pinch of salt. Blitz until completely smooth.

Transfer the cake mixture to the lined tin. Spoon over the blitzed date mixture, swirling it into the cake mixture.Bake for 40 minutes, until just set in the centre and an inserted skewer comes out clean. Remove and leave to cool in the tin for 15 minutes then turn out onto a wire cooling rack to cool completely.

If you want to serve the cake with drizzled chocolate, place the chocolate in a small heatproof bowl over a pan of barely simmering water, ensuring the base of the bowl does not come into contact with the water. Stir now and again until the chocolate has melted.

Serve the cake in thin slices with yoghurt or ice cream, and a little drizzle of melted chocolate if you like. Keep for up to 4 days in an airtight container.

BAKED RICE PUDDING

SERVES 4–6

You may think of rice pudding and shudder as it brings back horrid memories of sloppy school dinners or congealed milk. Well, rid yourself of those thoughts and get ready for this very creamy yet dairy-free recipe. Combining my favourite flavours of orange and chocolate I'm happy to say this pudding is light yet creamy with not a dinner lady in sight.

450ml oat milk

80ml maple syrup

2 tbsp chickpea (gram or besan) flour

1 tbsp ground flax seeds

1 orange

400g cooked brown rice (freshly cooked from 200g raw rice or from a ready to eat pouch)

100g dark chocolate, minimum 70% cocoa solids, broken into small pieces

1 vanilla pod, cut in half lengthways

Non-dairy ice cream or yoghurt, to serve (optional)

Preheat the oven to 160°C/140°C fan/325°F/gas mark 3.

In a bowl whisk together the milk, maple syrup, chickpea flour and ground flax seeds. Finely grate the zest from half the orange and peel strips of zest from the other half. Add both the grated zest and peeled zest into the mixture with the brown rice. Stir to combine.

Pour half the mixture into a medium casserole dish. Scatter over the dark chocolate pieces then cover with the remaining rice and place the vanilla pod on top.

Bake for 45 minutes until set and golden on top. Remove the vanilla pod. Serve immediately with ice cream or yoghurt, if you like.

MAPLE, DATE AND HAZELNUT TART

MAKES 1 X 20CM ROUND CAKE, SERVES 10–12

It can sometimes be tricky to get a good vegan tart base recipe but you should find this recipe works well and it's also full of wonderful nutty flavour. The topping is so thick and creamy that I usually close my eyes with each bite and drift off momentarily . . .

For the base
130g blanched hazelnuts
100g oat cakes
90g pitted Medjool dates
3 tbsp coconut oil
Pinch of sea salt
Sunflower oil, for greasing

For the topping
225g avocado flesh
100g pitted Medjool dates
100g coconut oil, melted
2 tbsp hazelnut or cashew
  butter
70ml maple syrup
50g cacao or cocoa powder
Pinch of sea salt

Special equipment needed
20cm round springform tin

Preheat the oven to 200°C/180°C fan/400°F/gas mark 6. Brush the tin with sunflower oil.

Place the hazelnuts on a tray and roast for 5-7 minutes, until a shade darker and aromatic, taking care not to let them burn. Remove and leave to cool.

Once cool, add 80g of the hazelnuts to a food processor with the remaining base ingredients and blitz until finely ground and the mixture sticks together when pressed between your fingers. Press very firmly into the tin so you have an even, smooth base. Place in the fridge to set for 30 minutes or the freezer for 15 minutes.

For the topping, put all the ingredients into a food processor and blitz for a few minutes until completely smooth and creamy. Pour the mixture over the base and return to the fridge to set for one hour or the freezer for 20 minutes.

Carefully transfer the tart onto a serving dish and position the remaining hazelnuts around the edge of the tart. Serve immediately. Keep refrigerated for up to 3 days in an airtight container.

DATE AND ALMOND CAKE WITH CARAMEL SAUCE

MAKES 1 X 23CM ROUND CAKE

This cake almost feels regal. It's rich and luxurious and is packed with fibre from the flax and the dates. It feels so moist due to the almonds and coconut oil too. Topped with the sauce, it's as close as you can get to pure heaven. The miso gives it such warmth and a dreamy richness and you can use this sauce in so many ways: pour it over cake, yoghurt or let your kids dip fruity kebabs into it as a little treat.

For the caramel
2 tbsp maple syrup
1 tbsp sunflower oil
2 tsp vanilla extract
1 tbsp white miso paste
3 tbsp coconut milk yoghurt

For the cake
3 tbsp ground flax seeds
130ml boiling water
100g pitted Medjool dates
75ml non-dairy milk
200g ground almonds
100g desiccated coconut
150g coconut palm sugar
150 coconut oil, melted
Zest of 1 lemon
1 tsp baking powder
¼ tsp sea salt
1 tsp vanilla extract
Non-dairy yoghurt, to serve

Special equipment needed
23cm round springform tin

Preheat the oven to 180°C/160°C fan/350°F/gas mark 4. Line the cake tin fully with baking parchment.

For the caramel, combine all the ingredients together in a bowl until completely smooth, cover and refrigerate.

In a small bowl, whisk together the ground flax seeds and water. Set aside for 2 minutes.

Place the dates in a food processor and add the flax seed mixture. Blitz to form a sticky paste. Add the milk, with the motor still running, and blitz until combined, then transfer to a large bowl.

Add the remaining cake ingredients to the food processor and mix until thoroughly combined. Pour the mixture into the cake tin and use the back of a spoon to level the surface. Bake in the centre of the oven for 25-30 minutes or until an inserted skewer comes out clean. If the top is browning too quickly, cover with foil. Remove and leave to cool in the tin for 10 minutes, then turn out onto a wire cooling rack to cool completely.

When ready to serve, stir the caramel and then drizzle over the cake. Serve with some yoghurt on the side. Keep any leftovers for up to 3 days in an airtight container.

AVOCADO, COCONUT AND CASHEW CHUNK ICE CREAM

SERVES 6

Luckily there are now lots of vegan ice creams available to buy and they taste just as good as regular ice cream. My kids often prefer the vegan ones as you can get some pretty out-there flavour combinations. As I've said many a time during this book it is always nicer to make something from scratch not only due to the freshness and flavour but also because it's such a lovely thing to do, to switch off one's phone and get stuck in to a practical task. Making your ice cream needn't be complicated and the feeling of satisfaction when you taste the results will be well worth the wait.

2 x 400ml tins full fat coconut cream

1 ripe avocado, halved and stoned

1 tsp vanilla paste

260ml maple syrup

100g cashews, roasted and roughly chopped

5 tbsp cashew butter

¼ tsp sea salt

Put the coconut cream, avocado, vanilla and 190ml of the maple syrup into a blender or processor and pulse on and off until completely smooth. Transfer to an airtight container or a shallow metal cake tin and cover with cling film, and carefully place in the freezer until completely frozen.

Meanwhile, in a bowl, mix the remaining maple syrup together with the chopped cashews, cashew butter, 3 tablespoons of boiling water and salt. Don't worry if it is not fully combined.

Once the ice cream is frozen, briefly run hot water over the base of the container or tin, just for a second or two, long enough to melt the outside of the ice cream, allowing you to dislodge the frozen slab from the tin and turn it out onto a chopping board. With a sharp knife, roughly chop the ice cream into chunks, then in batches, add to a blender or food processor and blitz until completely smooth.

Return the ice cream to the tin and swirl in the maple cashew mixture. Cover and return to the freezer for another 1-2 hours, or until just frozen. Serve in soft scoops. If you are making this in advance, be sure to remove the ice cream from the freezer at least 20-30 minutes before serving, to allow it to thaw a little so you can serve soft scoops.

TIPS AND TRICKS

If you are considering trying a vegan diet for a long period of time you may be feeling a little anxiety around changing up your usual eating patterns and have concerns about which switches to make and how you will shop. Hopefully this section will help you feel a little more at ease as you make those changes and less overwhelmed about what you can and can't eat.

If you love eggs and can't quite work out how you'll get your morning hit or protein or bind a delicious cake together then fear not. Tofu is one excellent egg alternative for your morning scramble, and bananas, chia or flax work well to bind bakes firmly together.

If you really don't want to forgo your morning buttered toast try using something else as a spread. Olive oil gives a Mediterranean feel, coconut oil at room temperature a little warmth and of course there are now many vegan spreads and butter alternatives available in most supermarkets and online.

Most shop-bought dough, whether it's filo or puff, are usually made with margarine so are completely vegan. You can easily whip up a pie or savoury snack with these shop-bought dough without a worry. The same goes for a lot of shop-bought biscuits. Always read the ingredients on the back of packs to see if margarine is used instead of butter.

If you're nervous about how you'll ever eat out again, get googling as vegan restaurants are now popping up all over the country and are serving some seriously great food. I've also noticed a big shift in how regular restaurants are catering for vegetarians and vegans and there are usually a good couple of options available. If you have little control over where you're eating due to a family celebration or outing, don't forget you can order several starters or sides to make up a main meal as most restaurants will have many good vegetable dishes on offer. Indian restaurants are always a good choice too as they excel in vegetarian and vegan cooking without it even being labelled in that way.

THINGS TO LOOK OUT FOR WHEN YOU'RE BUYING YOUR SUPERMARKET FAVOURITES

Going shopping as a vegan can be daunting, especially when you're buying packaged goods, but if you keep these points in mind, you'll be shopping like a vegan-pro in no time.

When you're checking food packets you might find that for some products there's no vegan-friendly label even though you can't see anything meat/dairy-related in the ingredients list. This is often because the factory the food comes from also makes products that aren't vegan, so they can't officially say the food is completely vegan-friendly. It's totally up to you whether you feel happy eating these products, but do make sure there are no sneaky non-vegan ingredients included – casein, L. Cysteine and whey are commonly used and derive from animal products.

Some wines and beers may have animal proteins or products, like isinglass, present so always check the label first.

Make sure you buy dry pasta as soft pasta has egg in it.

If you are partial to a bag of jelly sweets remember to look for vegan versions as the regular kind will have gelatine in which is a no go and the same goes for a lot of chewing gum.

Some crisps contain whey or animal enzymes so again it's important to check the packet first.

Lots of condiments are vegan-friendly, including most tomato ketchups, BBQ sauces and mustards but do watch out for mayonnaise – you'll need to get a vegan version if you can't do without it.

Speaking of condiments, the all-time brit favourite Worcester sauce contains anchovies so look for similar tasting vegan versions or ditch it from your shopping list altogether.

THANK YOU

I feel so lucky that I have had the opportunity to write *Happy Vegan*. Cooking, baking and learning more about food has become a full-time and much-loved hobby, so I'm grateful for being able to collate all of my new knowledge into this book.

First of all, thank YOU for picking up this book. Whether you're a fully-fledged long-term vegan; vegetarian who likes to dabble; meat eater who feels curious; or food lover who just adores hoarding cookbooks like I do – whatever your reason and flavour . . . thank you for feeling the pull towards this book.

A heartfelt thanks to Amanda Harris and Emily Barrett at Seven Dials for once again agreeing to publish me and for their ongoing support, understanding and light-handed prods when deadlines were calling. Your malleable and dynamic approach to work has helped me enormously and I'm forever grateful for that.

Jordan Bourke, you walking, talking, food encyclopaedia, how can I even begin to thank you on this one? I was nervous to delve into the vegan world professionally, but you boosted my confidence greatly and taught me so much along the way. I'm so proud of what we have created and there is no way I could have done it without you. You are the most talented chef out there!

Thank you to Holly Bott and Stuart the dog for totally 'getting me' and always pushing me in the right direction. Your energy and friendship mean the world to me. I'm just not so sure that Stuart is going to be convinced by vegan sausages!

Thanks to Sarah White, the most efficient person I've ever met. Without you, my life would be a bloody mess and you know it.

Thank you for your relentless organising all round.

Mary and baby Margot, thank you for being the most brilliant and powerful team: Mary, your guidance is always so valued and I'm so excited for what we can achieve together in the future; and baby Margot, well done on being so blinking beautiful.

Rowan! Thank you so much for helping me continue my publishing adventure. You're an inspiration to little Kit and have surely created the most dedicated little bookworm out there. Working mum vibes all round. You rock.

Andrew, it was lovely working with you and your team for the first time. The photos of the food look sensational and our shoot for the cover was fun and laid back which is always a treat! The photography also looks very pretty due to the talents of Jo Harris and her beady eye for style and detail. Thank you for making each shot in this book look sublime.

Ru Merritt, Helen Ewing, Clare Sivell and Claire Keep who complete the creative and production team at Orion – thank you for all your hard work and dedication.

Jesse Wood, my best mate, husband and father to my scrummy kids, thank you for trying out all these dishes when some nights you really just wanted a Deliveroo. I love you. Arthur and Lola, my brilliant stepchildren, I promise I'll make some cakes with real butter and egg in for you soon. Rex and Honey, my sweet babies, thank you for being you. I'm one lucky mumma/stepmum. I love you all.

Lastly, thank you to Eric Findlay for inspiring me so much with his positivity, unique way of looking at life and selflessness. Missed beyond belief but still shining his light into our lives with his magic.

INDEX

apple
    Date and turmeric spiced
        breakfast smoothie 35
    Festive chocolate almond loaf
        181
    Jackfruit burgers and slaw 145
    Mince pies 182
Apple cider beetroot soup 64
apricot
    Apricot and raspberry slices 41
    Festive chocolate almond loaf
        181
    Spiced chocolate and cashew
        squares 174
aubergine
    Charred aubergine with tahini
        and herbs 155
    No pigs in blankets 170
avocado
    Avocado, coconut and cashew
        chunk ice cream 215
    Banana, avocado and
        chocolate loaf 198
    Breakfast smoothie bowls 37
    Cauliflower rice salad with
        cannellini beans, avocado
        and radishes 74
    Homemade baked beans 34
    Indian spiced potatoes and
        raita on toast 31
    Pepper, avocado, black bean
        and rice burritos 87
    Quinoa nori rolls 73
    The ultimate vegan sandwich
        66
    Vegan nachos 57

Baked chocolate orange rice
    pudding 208
banana
    Banana and almond butter
        cookies 204
    Banana, avocado and
        chocolate loaf 198
    Banana pancakes 23
    Breakfast smoothie bowls 37

Cashew, pear and chocolate
    baked oats 24
    Date and turmeric spiced
BBQ broccoli bites 169
breakfast smoothie 35
beans
    Vegan nachos 57
black
    Black bean and tomato sweet
        potatoes 160
    Black bean sausages 126
    Mixed bean chilli with
        flatbreads 151
    No pigs in blankets 170
    Pepper, avocado, black bean
        and rice burritos 87
black-eyed
    Tomato, fennel and bean bake
        123
broad
    Warm pea, broad bean and
        pine nut pasta salad 63
butter
    Miso butter beans with quinoa
        77
    Spicy bean stew 156
cannellini
    Blueberry and cannellini bean
        tray bake 197
    Cauliflower rice salad with
        cannellini beans, avocado
        and radishes 74
edamame
    Butternut squash, edamame
        and spinach grain bowl 114
haricot
    Homemade baked beans 34
kidney
    Mixed bean chilli with
        flatbreads 151
    Piri piri tofu 94
    Rice and veggie bowl 84
    Spicy bean stew 156
runner
    Runner beans with red onion,
        red pepper and tomato
        sauce 83
beetroot
    Apple cider beetroot soup 64

Beetroot falafel 93
Beetroot, tahini and chestnut
    dip 53
The ultimate vegan sandwich
    66
Black bean and tomato sweet
    potatoes 160
Blueberry and cannellini bean
    tray bake 197
bread
    Easy seeded bread 19
Breakfast smoothie bowls 37
broccoli
    BBQ broccoli bites 169
    Broccoli katsu curry 124
    Curried lentil, tenderstem
        broccoli, spring onion and
        red pepper salad 135
    Ginger and miso tofu with
        noodles 132
    Piri piri tofu 94
Butternut squash, edamame and
    spinach grain bowl 114

Caramelised butternut squash
    with balsamic roasted
    tomatoes 152
carrot
    Black bean sausages 126
    Broccoli katsu curry 124
    Carrot, cumin and coconut
        soup 70
    Jackfruit burgers and slaw
        145
    Mixed root mash 128
    Moroccan chickpea and lentil
        stew 113
    Orange roasted carrots 147
    Squash, lentil, mushroom and
        thyme casserole 109
    Sweet potato dumpling topped
        vegetable pie 164
    The ultimate vegan sandwich
        66
    Tomato, fennel and bean bake
        123
    Vegetable kofta wraps 100
Cashew, pear and chocolate
    baked oats 24

cauliflower
  Cauliflower rice salad with
    cannellini beans, avocado
    and radishes 74
  Cauliflower steaks with pine
    nut and parsley oil 140
  Charred spiced cauliflower with
    spring onions and sesame
    seeds 163
  Creamy new potato, cauliflower
    and turmeric bake 110
  Vegetable kofta wraps 100
cavolo nero
  Italian braised chickpeas with
    cavolo nero and rosemary
    104
Charred aubergine with tahini and
    herbs 155
Charred spiced cauliflower with
    spring onions and sesame
    seeds 163
chickpea
  Baked chocolate orange rice
    pudding 208
  Beetroot falafel 93
  Flatbread pizzas with basil and
    chickpea pesto, rocket and
    cherry tomatoes 120
  Italian braised chickpeas with
    cavolo nero and rosemary
    104
  Moroccan chickpea and lentil
    stew 113
  Vegetable kofta wraps 100
Chinese-style dumplings 96
Chinese-style tofu, cucumber and
    cashew salad 69
chocolate
  Baked chocolate orange rice
    pudding 208
  Banana, avocado and
    chocolate loaf 198
  Chocolate and strawberry chia
    squares 45
  Chocolate fudge cake 207
  Chocolate Halloween spiders
    178
  Chocolate orange mousse 190

Doughnut balls with chocolate
    and date sauce 202
No bake chocolate peanut
    butter cookies 46
Spiced chocolate and cashew
    squares 174
Tahini fudge brownies 194
coconut, desiccated
  Chocolate orange mousse 190
  Date and almond cake with
    caramel sauce 213
  Paradise porridge 20
courgette
  Chinese-style dumplings 96
  Fried courgette with roasted
    peppers, peanuts and chilli
    129
Creamy new potato, cauliflower
    and turmeric bake 110
Curried lentil, tenderstem
    broccoli, spring onion and
    red pepper salad 135

date
  Chocolate and strawberry chia
    squares 45
  Chocolate fudge cake 207
  Chocolate Halloween spiders
    178
  Date and almond cake with
    caramel sauce 213
  Date and turmeric spiced
    breakfast smoothie 35
  Doughnut balls with chocolate
    and date sauce 202
  Maple, date and hazelnut tart
    210
Doughnut balls with chocolate
    and date sauce 202

Easy seeded bread 19
Espresso notini 184

fennel, bulb
  Tomato, fennel and bean bake
    123
Festive chocolate almond loaf
    181

Flatbread pizzas with basil and
    chickpea pesto, rocket and
    cherry tomatoes 120
Flatbreads with hummus,
    sundried tomatoes and
    olives 79
French toast with peaches and
    cashew drizzle 27
Fried courgette with roasted
    peppers, peanuts and chilli
    129

Garlic and pak choi fried rice 136
Ginger and miso tofu with
    noodles 132
Gingerbread people 177

Homemade baked beans 34

Iced lemon mint spritz 185
Indian spiced potatoes and raita
    on toast 31
Italian braised chickpeas with
    cavolo nero and rosemary 104

Jackfruit burgers and slaw 145

lentil
  Curried lentil, tenderstem
    broccoli, spring onion and
    red pepper salad 135
  Moroccan chickpea and lentil
    stew 113
  Pasta with lentil bolognese 103
  Tomato dahl with flatbreads 80
  Tomato, pesto and lentil baked
    peppers 91

Mac and cashew cheese 99
Maple, date and hazelnut tart 210
Mince pies 182
miso
  Coconut cream spinach pasta
    119
  Creamy new potato, cauliflower
    and turmeric bake 110
  Date and almond cake with
    caramel sauce 213

Ginger and miso tofu with noodles 132
Mac and cashew cheese 99
Miso butter beans with quinoa 77
Miso caramel popcorn 173
Miso scrambled tofu and avocado on rye 28
Quinoa nori rolls 73
Rice and veggie bowl 84
Sweet potato rostis 32
Sweet potato wedges with creamy spinach dip 55
The ultimate vegan sandwich 66
Tomato dahl with flatbreads 80
Vegan cheesy dip 56
Mixed bean chilli with flatbreads 151
Mixed root mash 128
Moroccan chickpea and lentil stew 113
Multi seed crackers 52

No bake chocolate peanut butter cookies 46
No pigs in blankets 170
nuts (cashew, hazelnut, pecan, pine, etc.)
    Apricot and raspberry slices 41
    Avocado, coconut and cashew chunk ice cream 215
    Breakfast smoothie bowls 37
    Cashew, pear and chocolate baked oats 24
    Cauliflower steaks with pine nut and parsley oil 140
    Chinese-style tofu, cucumber and cashew salad 69
    Chocolate Halloween spiders 178
    Date and almond cake with caramel sauce 213
    Festive chocolate almond loaf 181
    Flatbread pizzas with basil and chickpea pesto, rocket and cherry tomatoes 120

Fried courgette with roasted peppers, peanuts and chilli 129
Mac and cashew cheese 99
Maple, date and hazelnut tart 210
Mince pies 182
Nut roast 146
Nutty brittle 173
Pear and pecan bircher muesli 14
Pomegranate and yoghurt cake 193
Rosemary and thyme spiced nuts 50
Spiced chocolate and cashew squares 174
Tomato, pesto and lentil baked peppers 91
Vegan cheesy dip 56
Warm pea, broad bean and pine nut pasta salad 63
Nutty brittle 173

oats
    Cashew, pear and chocolate baked oats 24
    Chocolate and strawberry chia squares 45
    Maple, date and hazelnut tart 210
    No bake chocolate peanut butter cookies 46
    Paradise porridge 20
    Pear and pecan bircher muesli 14
    Tofu fingers with sweet potato wedges 139
orange
    Baked chocolate orange rice pudding 208
    Chocolate orange mousse 190
    Festive chocolate almond loaf 181
    Mince pies 182
    Orange roasted carrots 147
    Pomegranate bomb 185

pak choi
    Garlic and pak choi fried rice 136
Paradise porridge 20
parsnip
    Nut roast 146
    Pasta with lentil bolognese 103
pea
    Sweet potato dumpling topped vegetable pie 164
    Vegetable kofta wraps 100
    Warm pea, broad bean and pine nut pasta salad 63
pepper, red
    Curried lentil, tenderstem broccoli, spring onion and red pepper salad 135
    Fried courgette with roasted peppers, peanuts and chilli 129
    Mixed bean chilli with flatbreads 151
    Pepper, avocado, black bean and rice burritos 87
    Piri piri tofu 94
    Quinoa nori rolls 73
    Runner beans with red onion, red pepper and tomato sauce 83
    Tomato, pesto and lentil baked peppers 91
peach
    French toast with peaches and cashew drizzle 27
pear
    Cashew, pear and chocolate baked oats 24
    Pear and pecan bircher muesli 14
Piri piri tofu 94
plum
    Upside down plum cake 200
Pomegranate and yoghurt cake 193
Pomegranate bomb 185
potato
    Creamy new potato, cauliflower and turmeric bake 110

Indian spiced potatoes and
raita on toast 31
Spinach and tomato gnocchi
106

quinoa
Miso butter beans with quinoa
77
Nutty brittle 173
Quinoa granola 16
Quinoa nori rolls 73

raspberry
Apricot and raspberry slices 41
Chocolate Halloween spiders
178
Raspberry and lemon scone
cake 42
Rice and veggie bowl 84
Rosemary and thyme spiced
nuts 50
Runner beans with red onion, red
pepper and tomato sauce 83

Sausage satay skewers 159
Sesame coated tofu 154
Spiced chocolate and cashew
squares 174
Spicy bean stew 156
spinach
Breakfast smoothie bowls 37
Butternut squash, edamame
and spinach grain bowl 114
Coconut cream spinach pasta
119
Date and turmeric spiced
breakfast smoothie 35
Miso butter beans with quinoa
77
Quinoa nori rolls 73
Spicy bean stew 156
Spinach and tomato gnocchi
106
Sweet potato wedges with
creamy spinach dip 55
squash
Butternut squash, edamame
and spinach grain bowl 114

Caramelised butternut squash
with balsamic roasted
tomatoes 152
Squash, lentil, mushroom and
thyme casserole 109
strawberry
chocolate and strawberry chia
squares 45
Strawberry chia jam 17
swede
Mixed root mash 128
sweet potato
Black bean and tomato sweet
potatoes 160
Mixed root mash 128
Nut roast 146
Rice and veggie bowl 84
Spicy bean stew 156
Squash, lentil, mushroom and
thyme casserole 109
Sweet potato dumpling topped
vegetable pie 164
Sweet potato rostis 32
Sweet potato wedges with
creamy spinach dip 55
Tofu fingers with sweet potato
wedges 139
Vegetable kofta wraps 100

tahini
Beetroot, tahini and chestnut
dip 53
Black bean and tomato sweet
potatoes 160
Blueberry and cannellini bean
tray bake 197
Chinese-style tofu, cucumber
and cashew salad 69
Coconut cream spinach pasta
119
Maple, date and hazelnut tart
210
Miso butter beans with quinoa
77
No pigs in blankets 170
Tahini and pomegranate fudge
49
Tahini fudge brownies 194

tofu
Black bean sausages 126
Chinese-style dumplings 96
Chinese-style tofu, cucumber
and cashew salad 69
Ginger and miso tofu with
noodles 132
Homemade baked beans 34
No pigs in blankets 170
Piri piri tofu 94
Quinoa nori rolls 73
Rice and veggie bowl 84
Sausage satay skewers 159
Sesame coated tofu 154
Sweet potato dumpling topped
vegetable pie 164
Sweet potato wedges with
creamy spinach dip 55
The ultimate vegan sandwich
66
Tofu fingers with sweet potato
wedges 139
Tofu tikka masala 131
tomato
Black bean and tomato sweet
potatoes 160
Black bean sausages 126
Butternut squash, edamame
and spinach grain bowl 114
Caramelised butternut squash
with balsamic roasted
tomatoes 152
Flatbread pizzas with basil and
chickpea pesto, rocket and
cherry tomatoes 120
Flatbreads with hummus,
sundried tomatoes and
olives 79
Homemade baked beans 34
Indian spiced potatoes and
raita on toast 31
Italian braised chickpeas with
cavolo nero and rosemary
104
Mixed bean chilli with
flatbreads 151
Moroccan chickpea and lentil
stew 113

No pigs in blankets 170
Pasta with lentil bolognese 103
Runner beans with red onion, red pepper and tomato sauce 83
Spicy bean stew 156
Spinach and tomato gnocchi 106
Sweet potato dumpling topped vegetable pie 164

Tofu tikka masala 131
Tomato dahl with flatbreads 80
Tomato, fennel and bean bake 123
Tomato, pesto and lentil baked peppers 91
Vegan nachos 57

Upside down plum cake 200

Vegan cheesy dip 56
Vegan nachos 57
Vegan sandwich, the ultimate 66
Vegetable kofta wraps 100

Warm pea, broad bean and pine nut pasta salad 63

OVEN TEMPERATURE GUIDE

	Elec °C	Elec °F	Elec °C (Fan)	Gas mark
Very cool	110	225	90	¼
Moderate	160	325	140	3
	170	350	160	4
Moderately hot	190	375	170	5
	200	400	180	6
Hot	220	425	200	7

LIQUID MEASUREMENTS (under 1 litre)

Metric	Imperial	Australian/US
60ml	2 fl oz	¼ cup
75ml	3 fl oz	
100ml	3½ fl oz	
120ml	4 fl oz	½ cup
150ml	5 fl oz	
180ml	6 fl oz	¾ cup
200ml	7 fl oz	
250ml	9 fl oz	1 cup
300ml	10½ fl oz	1¼ cups
350ml	12½ fl oz	1½ cups
400ml	14 fl oz	1¾ cups
450ml	16 fl oz	2 cups
600ml	1 pint	2½ cups
750ml	1¼ pints	3 cups
900ml	1½ pints	3½ cups

WEIGHT MEASUREMENTS

Metric	Imperial
10g	½ oz
20g	¾ oz
25g	1 oz
40g	1½ oz
50g	2 oz
60g	2½ oz
75g	3 oz
110g	4 oz
125g	4½ oz
150g	5 oz
175g	6 oz
200g	7 oz
225g	8 oz
250g	9 oz
275g	10 oz
350g	12 oz
450g	1lb
700g	1½ lb
900g	2lb

First published in Great Britain in 2019 by Seven Dials
An imprint of Orion Publishing Group Ltd
Carmelite House, 50 Victoria Embankment
London, EC4Y 0DZ
An Hachette UK Company

10 9 8 7 6 5 4 3 2 1

Text © Fearne Cotton 2019
Design and layout © Orion Publishing Group Ltd 2019

All rights reserved. No part of this publication
may be reproduced, stored in a retrieval system,
or transmitted in any form or by any means,
electronic, mechanical, photocopying, recording
or otherwise, without the prior permission of both
the copyright owner and the above publisher.

The right of Fearne Cotton to be identified as the
author of this work has been asserted in accordance
with the Copyright, Designs and Patents Act 1988.

A CIP catalogue record for this book
is available from the British Library.

ISBN (Hardback): 978 1 8418 8289 5
ISBN (eBook): 978 1 8418 8290 1

Publisher: Amanda Harris
Editors: Emily Barrett and Ru Merritt
Photography: Andrew Burton
Props: Jo Harris
Recipe development and food styling: Jordan Bourke
Art Direction and Design: Clare Sivell and Helen Ewing

Printed in Germany

Note: While every effort has been made to ensure
that the information in this book is correct, it should
not be substituted for medical advice. It is the sole
responsibility of the reader to determine which foods
are safe to consume. If you are concerned about any
aspect of your health, speak to your GP.

www.orionbooks.co.uk

MIX
Paper from
responsible sources
FSC® C011124